Ready, Set, Go!

A Student Guide to SPSS® 8.0 for Windows®

Thomas W. Pavkov
Kent A. Pierce

Purdue University Calumet

Mayfield Publishing Company
Mountain View, California
London • Toronto

Library of Congress Cataloging-in-Publication Data

Pavkov, Thomas W.
      Ready, set, go! : a student guide to SPSS 8.0 for Windows / Thomas
W. Pavkov, Kent A. Pierce.
        p.   cm.
      ISBN 0-7674-0515-3
      1. SPSS for Windows. 2. Social sciences—Statistical methods—
Computer programs. I. Pierce, Kent A.
      HA32.P3818   1998
      519.5'075'55369—dc21

                                                           98-8475
                                                           CIP

Manufactured in the United States of America
10 9 8 7 6 5 4 3 2 1

Mayfield Publishing Company
1280 Villa Street
Mountain View, CA 94041

Sponsoring editor, Franklin C. Graham; production editor, Julianna Scott Fein; manuscript editor, Thomas L. Briggs; design manager and cover designer, Susan Breitbard; art editor, Amy Folden; manufacturing manager, Randy Hurst; cover image, © Alán Gallegos/AG Photograph. The text was set in 11/14 Times by Archetype Book Composition and printed on acid-free 50# Butte des Morts by Banta Book Group.

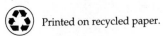 Printed on recycled paper.

Preface

This handbook provides the basic information students need to use SPSS® for Windows® in both introductory statistics and research design courses. When used in conjunction with a primary statistics or research design textbook, this book is a flexible and up-to-date tool instructors can use to incorporate computerized statistical analysis into their courses.

This book emerged from our need to provide students with basic information on using SPSS for Windows, the statistical package that we use as part of our course of instruction in behavioral statistics. After searching without success for a guide that would efficiently and clearly provide this type of information, we developed our own instructional material for the course. *Ready, Set, Go! A Student Guide to SPSS® for Windows®* is the result of our efforts. This handbook is an updated version designed for use with SPSS for Windows Version 8.0 or later.

This handbook is designed to be an inexpensive source of "how-to" information for student users of the SPSS for Windows software. Each assignment provides the user with background information linking statistical methods and the SPSS procedures associated with those methods. The steps of these procedures are illustrated by numerous screen shots of the SPSS graphical user interface. The book also provides basic information on the interpretation of output produced by SPSS. Each chapter ends with an "On Your Own" section with a learning task that encourages students to undertake independent computer assignments.

This book may be used for more than reference; each assignment has been developed as a guided exercise. Students are introduced to the research process as they work through exercises—formulating research questions, choosing appropriate statistical procedures, summarizing results, and interpreting data. We believe that this approach will help students understand the research process and increase their confidence in using SPSS datasets of their choice.

The book is organized topically, covering most of the basic concepts presented in introductory statistics courses. We begin with an assignment providing the student user with information on how to access basic SPSS procedures such as loading data and printing output. Assignments 2 and 3 cover SPSS procedures for descriptive statistics and for the graphical presentation of data. Assignments 4 through 7 focus on using SPSS to compare groups and paired-samples *t* tests and then move to one-way analysis of variance for independent and related samples. Correlation and regression analysis are covered in Assignments 8 and 9. Finally, in Assignment 10, the student user is introduced to using SPSS for producing contingency tables and calculating the chi-square statistic.

We wish to acknowledge the individuals at Mayfield Publishing Company for their support of this project. In particular, we would like to thank Frank Graham for his enthusiastic support of the concept. We would also like to thank Julianna Scott Fein, Susan Breitbard, Amy Folden, and Kim Russell. We would also like to thank our colleagues who reviewed this project in its earliest stages: Bruce Abbott (Indiana University–Purdue University at Fort Wayne), Dennis Berg (California State University–Fullerton), Kenneth Bordens (Indiana University–Purdue University at Fort Wayne), Bernardo Carducci (Indiana University Southeast), Paul C. Cozby (California State University–Fullerton), Bernard Gorman (Hofstra University), Louis Primavera (St. John's University), Steve Slane (Cleveland State University), B. Michael Thorne (Mississippi State University), and Todd Zakrajsek (Southern Oregon State College).

Contents

APPENDIX
Entering Data Using Programs Other Than SPSS   81

ASSIGNMENT 1
Learning the Basics of SPSS

OBJECTIVES

1. To learn how to load SPSS for Windows
2. To load a datafile into SPSS for Windows
3. To define SPSS variables
4. To obtain printouts from SPSS for Windows
5. To exit from SPSS for Windows

This section of the book will provide you with the information you need to use some of the basic procedures of SPSS for Windows. Access to SPSS for Windows varies from campus to campus and from computer to computer. The purpose of this book is to provide general information about the use of this software for student users of SPSS for Windows Version 8.0 or later. As you use SPSS, you may encounter some issues that are not covered by this book. In that case, you should seek assistance from your instructor or statistical consultant. For the student learning how to use SPSS for Windows, a number of general issues need to be addressed. Of primary importance is starting the software application. Next, you will need to know how to load data from an existing datafile, define data, and perhaps enter experimental data manually. You will also need to know how to print the results of your analysis following the completion of an SPSS procedure. These are the procedures you will learn in this section of the book.

STARTING SPSS

To start SPSS for Windows, you will need to start from your Windows Desktop; see Figure 1.1 for an example. Depending on your computer installation, you can access SPSS for Windows in different ways. You can start SPSS either by double-clicking on the SPSS Shortcut icon on the Windows Desktop or by pointing to the SPSS icon on the Windows Desktop menu of program listings (e.g., Start>Programs>SPSS).

After you double-click on the SPSS icon, the computer will load the SPSS software. You will know SPSS is loading when the Windows hourglass replaces

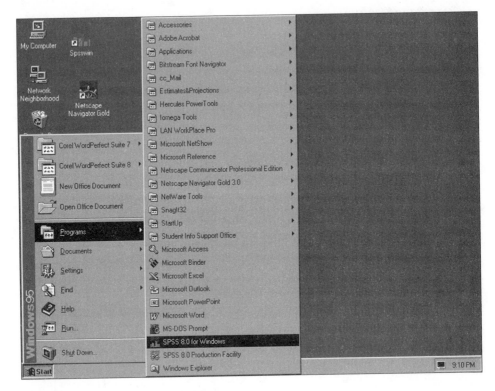

FIGURE 1.1   Windows Program Manager

the pointer on your screen. The time required to load SPSS varies depending on the characteristics of your computer. These factors include the power of your machine, the location or type of installation, and the load on network resources. You can enhance the performance of the machine you are using by making sure that other Windows applications are not running simultaneously with SPSS for Windows. If you find other applications loaded, unloading the applications prior to running SPSS may enhance performance.

LOADING A FILE

Upon completion of the loading process, you can initiate the loading of data for analysis. After you initiate the loading of the SPSS software, one of two series of screens appears, allowing you to initiate the data loading process. One method of loading data involves using the File pull-down menu, as in previous versions of SPSS for Windows. A second method involves using an optional dialog query

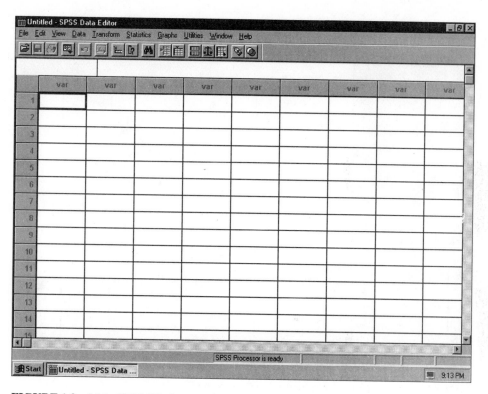

FIGURE 1.2   Main SPSS Window with Data Editor Window Active

window, which is new to SPSS for Windows Version 8.0. The method you use will depend on the way SPSS is installed at your location. Both methods are described in the following pages. If the dialog window is not in use at your location, a screen will appear that is similar to the screen shown in Figure 1.2. This screen is the active SPSS Data Editor window and the main SPSS for Windows screen. To load your data, point to the File menu and highlight one of the file loading options appearing on the window.

Figure 1.3 displays the selections available at the beginning of an SPSS session from the File pull-down menu. You have the choice of creating a new file, opening an existing file, or reading data from an ASCII (text) format file. As shown in Figure 1.3, the most recently accessed SPSS datasets are listed as well. You can access one of these files by simply pointing and single-clicking on the highlighted name of the file. You will use the Open option most often. In the pull-down menu, click on Open to open an existing file. In Figure 1.3, the Open choice

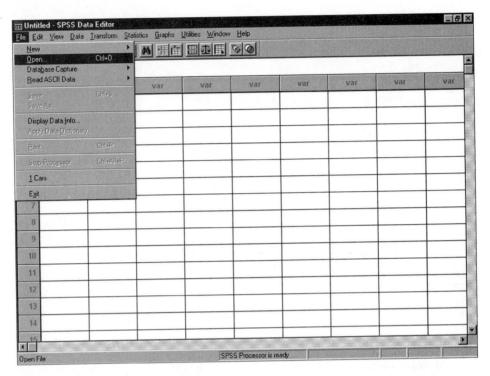

FIGURE 1.3   Opening a File from the SPSS File Menu

is highlighted. If you choose the File>Open option, the SPSS Open File window will appear next (see Figure 1.5).

The second method of opening a datafile involves using a Windows dialog box, as shown in Figure 1.4. If your installation uses the dialog option, this box will appear along with the SPSS Data Editor in the background. This dialog window allows you to access the SPSS tutorial, type in data using the Data Editor window, create or run a query using a database table, or open an existing SPSS datafile. If you choose to use this dialog box in the future, you are most likely to use the default Open an existing file option. Recently accessed files are listed in the small box under this option. You can access one of these files by highlighting and double-clicking on the file. SPSS will then load the file, and data will appear in the SPSS Data Editor (see Figure 1.6). If the datafile you wish to access does not appear on the list, highlight and double-click on More Files. Then you can access your datafile using the Open File window, as illustrated in Figure 1.5. If you do not wish to use this dialog box in the future, click on the check-box in the lower part of the dialog window titled Don't show this dialog in the future.

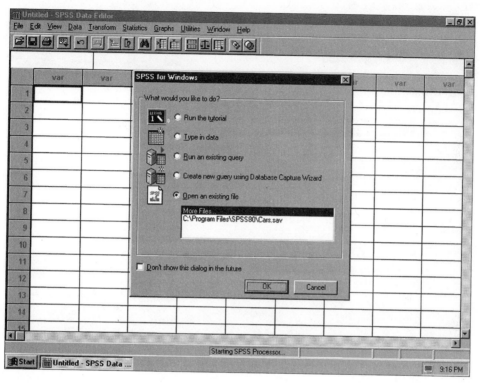

FIGURE 1.4   SPSS for Windows Optional Dialog Box

USING THE Open File WINDOW

Once you select Open, the Open File window appears. Because thousands of files may be stored in the computer system, you will need to identify the location and name of the dataset you are going to use in the assignment. The Open File window allows you to direct SPSS in accessing named datasets. As shown in Figure 1.5, the Look in box at the top of the window shows the active folder. The active folder corresponds with the directory or sub-directory to which SPSS for Windows is pointed. You can change the directory to which SPSS for Windows is pointed by simply clicking on the down arrow at the right-hand side of the Look in box. You can also change directories by pointing and clicking on the device or directory you want to access by clicking on the Folder button.

The large box in the middle of the Open File window contains the names of the files contained in active folder. Figure 1.5 shows a list of files stored in the SPSS folder. To load one of these files, you must first highlight it and then point and click on the Open button or simply point and double-click on the highlighted file.

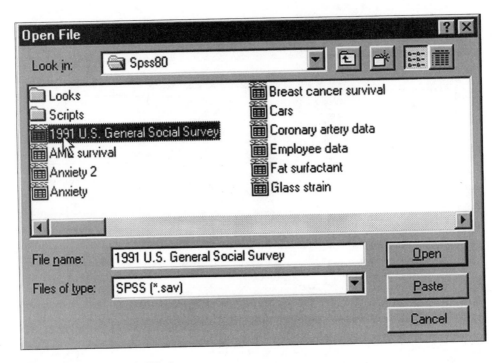

FIGURE 1.5   Open File Window

Notice in Figure 1.5 that SPSS automatically looks for files with the extension .sav as designated in the Files of type box at the bottom of the Open File window. These files are referred to as SPSS Save (.sav) files and contain data stored in a compressed binary format. To complete the assignment, you will need to identify the appropriate Save file, select that file, and load it. Your instructor will inform you which file (along with directory/folder location) to use as he or she makes each computer assignment. Once you locate the correct folder (see Figure 1.5), SPSS will automatically list the Save files in the large box in the middle of the window. In this particular example, the datafile named 1991 U.S. General Social Survey subset is highlighted. This file is located in the SPSS folder. Once you highlight it, you can load the file by pointing and clicking on the Open button or by pointing and double-clicking on the highlighted file.

    Note that you can select other types of files. By pointing and clicking on the down arrow in the Files of type box, you can list a number of other file types in the large box, including a variety of database and spreadsheet formats. Generally, however, you will open only two other types of files. You can open the SPSS

Syntax files to analyze problems with SPSS syntax. (SPSS Syntax files are usually saved with the file extension designation of .sps. These files contain the actual SPSS program language needed to run your SPSS assignments.) You can also open SPSS Viewer files to examine and print the output from your SPSS assignments. These files are usually saved with the file extension designation of .spo. SPO files contain the information produced by SPSS statistical procedures. After you have directed SPSS to load a file, note the bottom bar on the SPSS window. This bar is called the status bar and will inform you of the status of the SPSS program during processing. When you are loading data, the SPSS status bar tells you that it is getting the file you have requested. SPSS also tells you the number of cases it is reading from the file as the datafile is loaded into memory. After the datafile is loaded, the SPSS status bar will inform you that the SPSS Processor is ready (see Figure 1.6).

THE PULL-DOWN MENUS

Examine the SPSS Data Editor window, as illustrated in Figure 1.6. There are a number of pull-down menus across the top, and a toolbar with various icons appears below the menu bar. To operate the menus, use the mouse to point and then click on the menu to which you have pointed. To activate a procedure represented by an icon, point to the icon and click on it.

For most of the computer assignments in this book, you will work with the File, Data, and Statistics menus. These menus contain the choices you will use for general operations (calling up or creating a datafile), for definitions of data (learning about variables contained in a pre-existing datafile or defining data entered manually), and for statistical operations (calling up a particular statistical procedure for analysis). The File menu also contains the commands for printing output from your SPSS analysis.

Take some time to familiarize yourself with the characteristics of these pull-down menus. Notice that after you single-click and then move the pointer from one selection to the next, a pull-down menu appears under each selection. Also notice that some menus are connected to sub-menus. These menus will appear when you point to a procedure that contains multiple sub-procedures. You will use some of these procedures and sub-procedures while working on the computer assignments in this book. Given the wide range of statistical procedures available in SPSS for Windows, however, you will probably not use all of the procedures. In terms of sophistication, many of these statistical procedures go far beyond the scope of this text and require specialized statistical expertise.

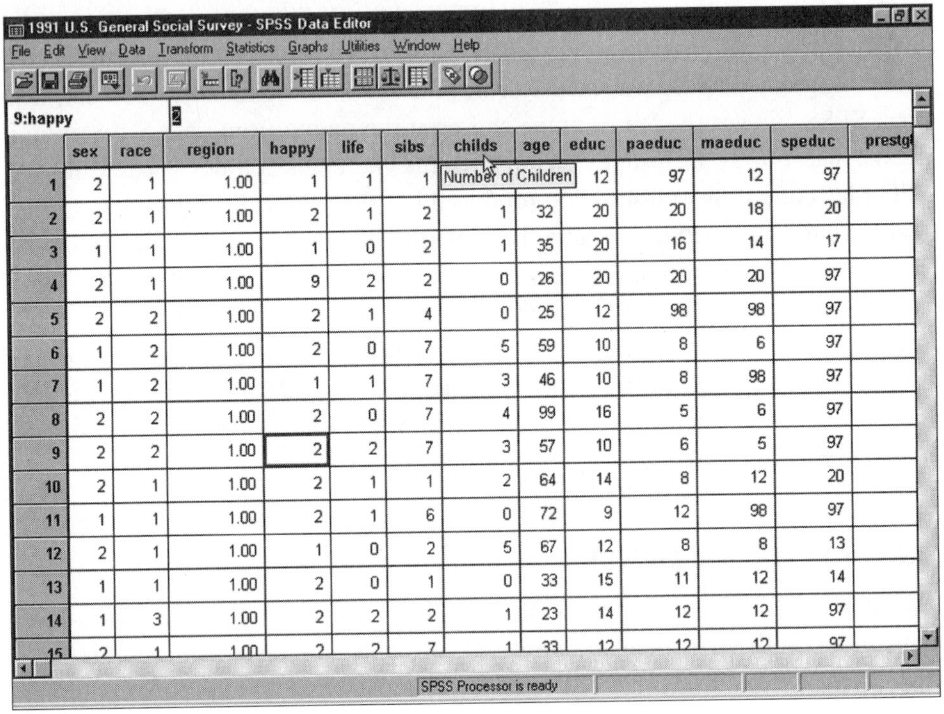

	sex	race	region	happy	life	sibs	childs	age	educ	paeduc	maeduc	speduc	prestg
1	2	1	1.00	1	1	1			12	97	12	97	
2	2	1	1.00	2	1	2	1	32	20	20	18	20	
3	1	1	1.00	1	0	2	1	35	20	16	14	17	
4	2	1	1.00	9	2	2	0	26	20	20	20	97	
5	2	2	1.00	2	1	4	0	25	12	98	98	97	
6	1	2	1.00	2	0	7	5	59	10	8	6	97	
7	1	2	1.00	1	1	7	3	46	10	8	98	97	
8	2	2	1.00	2	0	7	4	99	16	5	6	97	
9	2	2	1.00	2	2	7	3	57	10	6	5	97	
10	2	1	1.00	2	1	1	2	64	14	8	12	20	
11	1	1	1.00	2	1	6	0	72	9	12	98	97	
12	2	1	1.00	1	0	2	5	67	12	8	8	13	
13	1	1	1.00	2	0	1	0	33	15	11	12	14	
14	1	3	1.00	2	2	2	1	23	14	12	12	97	
15	2	1	1.00	2	2	7	1	33	12	12	12	97	

FIGURE 1.6 SPSS Data Editor Window After Data from a File Is Loaded

DATA DEFINITION WITH VARIABLE LABELS AND VALUE LABELS

When you complete the data loading process, a screen similar to that shown in Figure 1.6 will appear. Numbers will appear in what looks like a spreadsheet. These numbers are your actual data. The rows in the spreadsheet correspond to one case in the study (note the numbers in the left-most column). The columns in the spreadsheet correspond to one variable measured in the study. At the top of each column of numbers is a label (e.g., educ and age). These are your variable names.

Note that you can move the active cell (i.e., the cell in the spreadsheet shown with double-thick black lines) around the spreadsheet using the arrow keys on the keyboard. Or you can use the mouse to place the active cell by pointing and clicking on the cell to which you want to move. When moving the active cell around the spreadsheet, avoid making keystrokes on the computer keyboard, because you might accidentally change a value in the spreadsheet. As shown in Figure 1.6, pointing at the variable name will cause the variable label to appear below the variable name. This feature is useful in attempting to quickly understand variable definitions.

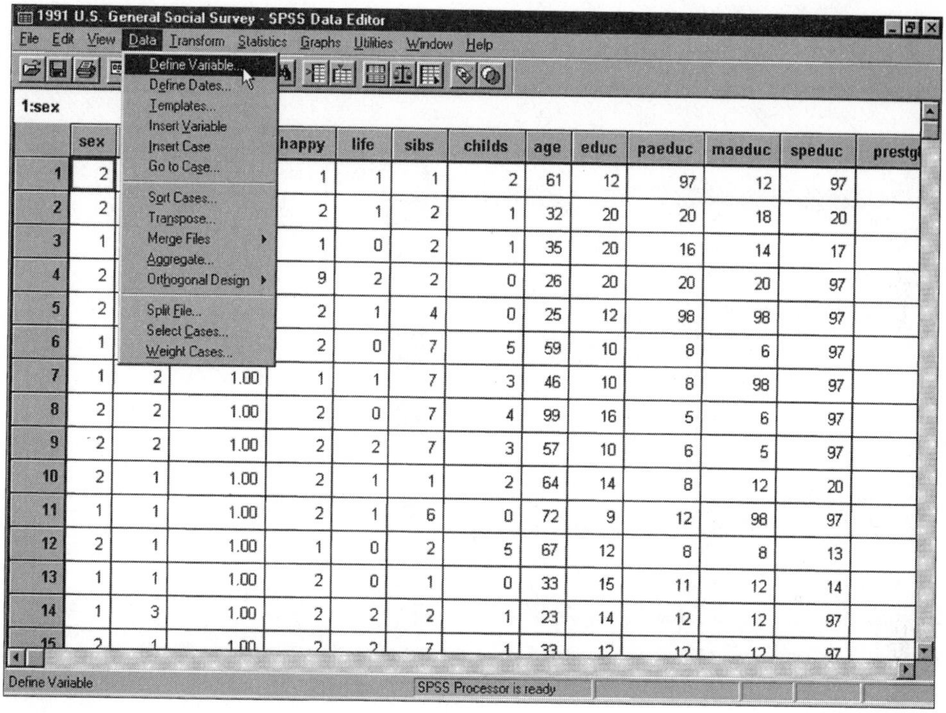

FIGURE 1.7   Choosing the Define Variable Window

DATA DEFINITION

Data definition is an important function in the analysis of data. Data definition provides documentation about the data in a file being used or created. Generally, each variable in a datafile has two sets of labels, which describe what the variable is measuring and what values are associated with the measure. In many datafiles, variable and value labels are predefined and stored in the *.sav file. In some situations, however, you will want to enter your own data for analysis using SPSS. In this case, you will have to provide your own variable and value labels. Regardless of the situation, you will need to access the data definition procedure in SPSS. Highlight the Data>Define Variable pull-down menu as shown in Figure 1.7 to start the process of data definition.

Once you have highlighted the Define Variable option from the Data pull-down menu, a second window will appear (as shown in Figure 1.7), called the Define Variable window. This window provides information about the variable you have chosen in the SPSS Data window. (The variable was chosen by pointing to the column with the mouse and then clicking on the column. Note the shading of

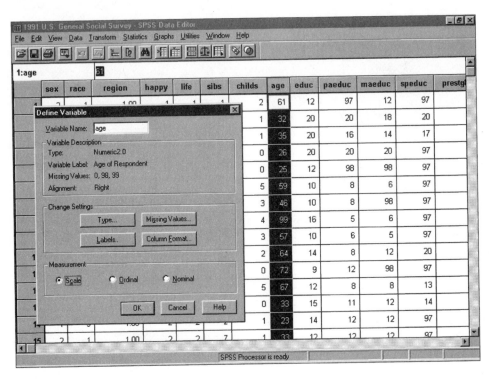

FIGURE 1.8   Define Variable Window

the age variable column under the active cell located on the first row of data in Figure 1.8.)

The Define Variable window allows you to perform a number of tasks. If you are using a predefined SPSS datafile, it allows you to examine variable attributes. If you are creating your own datafiles, it allows you to define your variables. It also allows you to define your scale of measurement as nominal, ordinal, or scale (ratio or interval) and to define missing values and column formats. This book will focus on datafiles with variable and value labels predefined by SPSS.

When using predefined datafiles, a researcher will often want to examine how the variables are stored because SPSS can store them in a number of formats. In most instances, you will encounter variables in predefined datafiles that are stored as numerics, such as the age variable in Figure 1.8. You might also encounter variables that are stored as characters, dates, or times or in currency formats. If you are generating your own data, however, you will not be using a pre-existing datafile. Instead, you will collect your data and create your own datafile in SPSS. You might also enter or retrieve data from a word processor such as Microsoft Word,

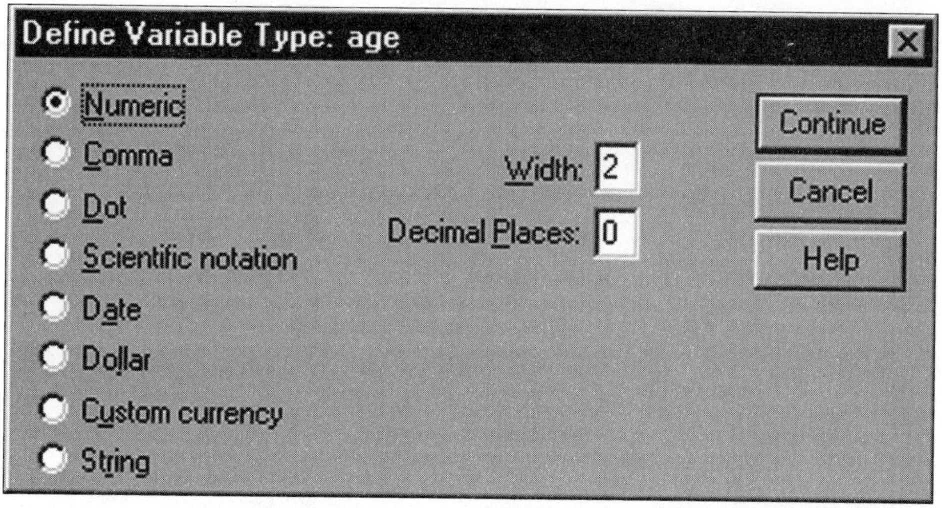

FIGURE 1.9 Define Variable Type Window

from spreadsheet software like Excel or Lotus, or from a database like dBase or Access (see the Appendix). SPSS has the capability of reading data from all these sources.

On the other hand, you might prefer to enter your data directly into SPSS using the spreadsheet that appears in the SPSS Data Editor window. To enter data into SPSS using the Data window, you must define each variable entered into the file. You can define the variable by clicking on the Type button in the Data Definition window. After you click on the Type button, the Define Variable Type window will appear, as shown in Figure 1.9. This window allows you to define how the variable is stored in the datafile, as well as the size of the variable. In the case of the age variable, Figure 1.9 shows the variable being stored as a numeric variable with a width of 2 spaces and 0 decimal places. If your instructor requires you to enter data, you will need to define each of the variables in the datafile you are creating.

Whether using a predefined datafile or an original, researchers use both variable and value labels to further define their variables. To access these labels, click on the Labels button in the Data Definition window. After you click on the Labels button, the Define Labels window will appear, as shown in Figure 1.10. This window gives information on the variables contained in predefined datafiles and also enables you to define your own variable and value labels using the Add, Change, and Remove buttons. Both variable and value labels will appear for datafile variables in this window.

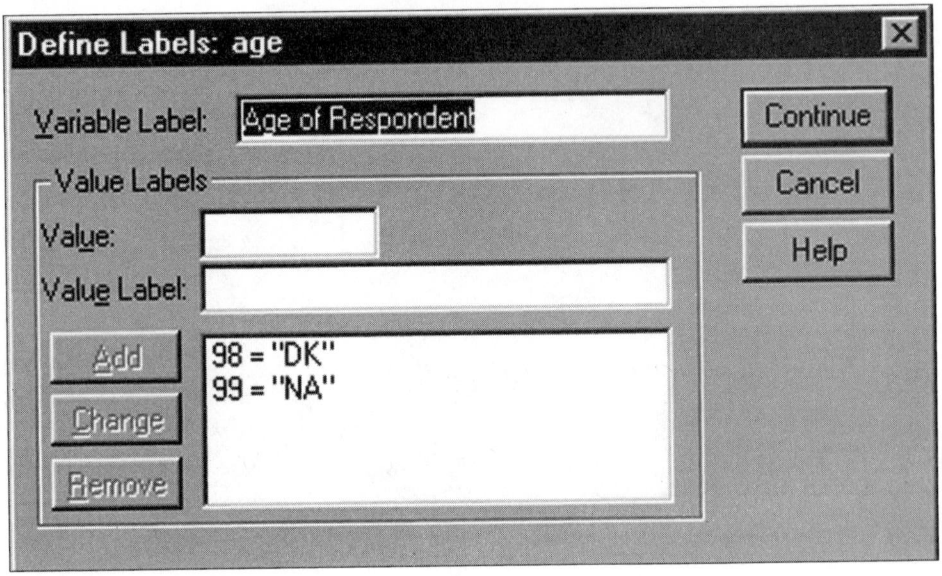

FIGURE 1.10   Define Labels Window

VIEWING SPSS OUTPUT

SPSS will display the output in the SPSS Viewer screen. Upon completion of SPSS processing, the SPSS Viewer screen automatically appears as the active window on your computer monitor, as shown in Figure 1.11. Note that the SPSS Viewer window has two large display panes, each having scrollbars. The left-hand pane is referred to as the Viewer Outline pane and contains an outline showing the structure of the SPSS output. Specifically, this outline contains information on the type of SPSS procedure performed, the title of the output, notes on the SPSS procedure including program syntax, and the requested statistical output. The right-hand pane contains information in the form of tables, charts, and text produced by SPSS statistical procedures. You can navigate the SPSS output in this pane by pointing and clicking on the element you wish to examine in the left-hand pane. In Figure 1.11, the Statistics portion of the outline is highlighted, and a corresponding arrow with a box is displayed in the right-hand pane. You can move the output on the computer screen by clicking on the arrows that appear on the scrollbars on the right-hand side and at the bottom of the Output screen. These arrows will reposition the output in both panes so that you can examine the entire content of either pane. At any point during your SPSS session, you can also examine your SPSS output by highlighting SPSS Viewer in the Window pull-down menu (i.e., Window>Outputl -SPSS Viewer).

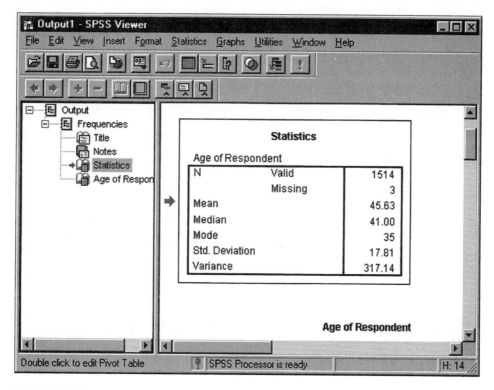

FIGURE 1.11   Active SPSS Viewer Window

Note that the SPSS output contains a number of items. As shown in Figure 1.12, in addition to the results of your requested SPSS procedures, the Notes section of output contains information on SPSS syntax and information on errors. You will find this information helpful in troubleshooting problems you encounter using SPSS.

PRINTING SPSS OUTPUT

After viewing your SPSS output, you can print the output or save the output to a file. To obtain a printout of your SPSS output, you will need to access the File pull-down menu. Figure 1.13 shows the location of the Print command in the File menu. Using the File menu, select the File>Print option.

After you point and click on the Print option, the Print window will appear, as shown in Figure 1.14. The Print window contains a number of printing options. In the Name box section of the Print window, the default printer device is indicated. If the default printer is the printer you wish to use, you can execute the Print function

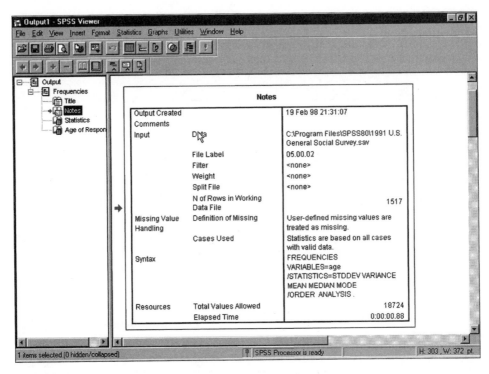

FIGURE 1.12   Active SPSS Viewer Window Showing Notes

by pointing and clicking on the OK button at the bottom of the window. This will result in a printout of the SPSS output file on a printer linked to your machine or network. If the output file is large, a few minutes may pass before it begins printing. The Print window allows you several options related to choosing a printer, specifying the style of printed output and the number and collation of copies, and printing the output to a file. You can change the printer by pointing and clicking on the down arrow appearing in the box. A list of available printing devices will appear. You can choose another printing device simply by pointing and clicking on that device.

You can specify the style of printout by pointing and clicking on the Properties button. After you point and click on the Properties button, the Properties window will appear. You can choose among a variety of print options appearing in the window, including portrait or landscape print layouts. Pointing and clicking on the Print to File box will cause a checkmark to appear in the box. After you point and click on the OK button with the checkmark indicated, the Print to file window will appear, allowing you to name the output file and folder for storage. The Number of copies box allows you to specify the desired number of copies either by inserting

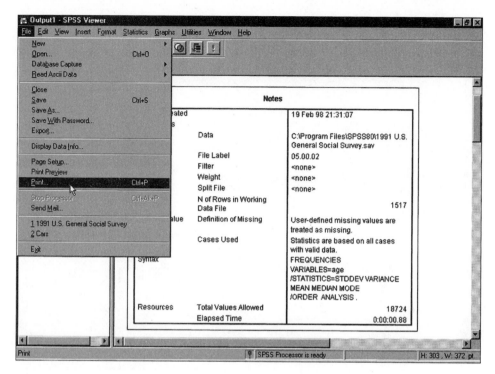

FIGURE 1.13 Selecting the Print Option from an Active SPSS Viewer Window

the number desired or by increasing or decreasing the value in the box using the up and down arrows. When the value appearing in the box is greater than 1, SPSS allows you to print output in a collated form.

Note that it is very important to request a printout of output from an active SPSS Viewer window. Requesting a printout from an active SPSS Data Editor window will cause SPSS to print the entire datafile. If you are using a large datafile, you will obtain many pages of useless printout!

EXITING SPSS

If you are using SPSS on a campus computer, unloading the SPSS program is a matter of computer courtesy! Once you complete your data analysis, you will need to exit the SPSS program. Access the File pull-down menu and highlight Exit. SPSS will begin the software unloading process. SPSS will prompt you to save your working datafile and update changes made to the file after you answer yes to the query. SPSS will also prompt you to save the SPSS Viewer window and will save the output file to the filename that you choose. After saving these files, SPSS will unload, and the Windows Desktop screen will reappear.

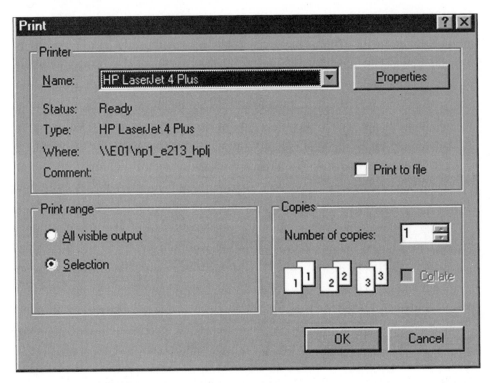

FIGURE 1.14   Specifying Print Options from the Print Window

ON YOUR OWN

You are now familiar with the basics of SPSS for Windows. To gain some experience, do the following:

1. Load SPSS, and then load the datafile you will use in your course.

2. Using the data definition facility, describe two of the variables in your datafile in terms of what they measure and what values are used in the measurement.

3. Take notes on any problems you encountered in accessing SPSS, and report them to your instructor.

Anxiety 2: Growth Study
* do 2 more times w/ different sets of data

ASSIGNMENT 2

Looking at Frequency Distributions and Descriptive Statistics

---

OBJECTIVES

1. To produce a frequency distribution

2. To use SPSS to calculate measures of central tendency

3. To use SPSS to calculate the variance of a distribution

4. To obtain a printout of SPSS output showing your work

5. To describe the data as shown in SPSS output

This assignment is your first do-it-yourself experience with SPSS. In this assignment, you will learn how to explore your data using the SPSS Frequencies procedure.

Researchers often explore their data before actually using statistical procedures in the hypothesis testing process. Why would you want to explore your data? The main goal is to understand the distribution of data. You should be interested in characteristics of the data such as the shapes of the distributions, the central tendencies of the distributions, and the variance of the distributions.

To explore the data, however, you must first organize the data into a comprehensible form. This allows you to easily and effectively communicate any trends evident in the data. The statistical methods used in organizing and presenting data are often referred to as descriptive statistics. To apply these statistical methods, you will use the Frequencies procedure to produce frequency distributions and calculate measures of central tendency and variance. By using this procedure and SPSS graphics, you will be able to present properties of the distribution using a variety of graphical presentations.

USING THE Frequencies PROCEDURE

You will access the Frequencies procedure after starting SPSS. As described in Assignment 1, start SPSS either by double-clicking on the SPSS Shortcut icon in

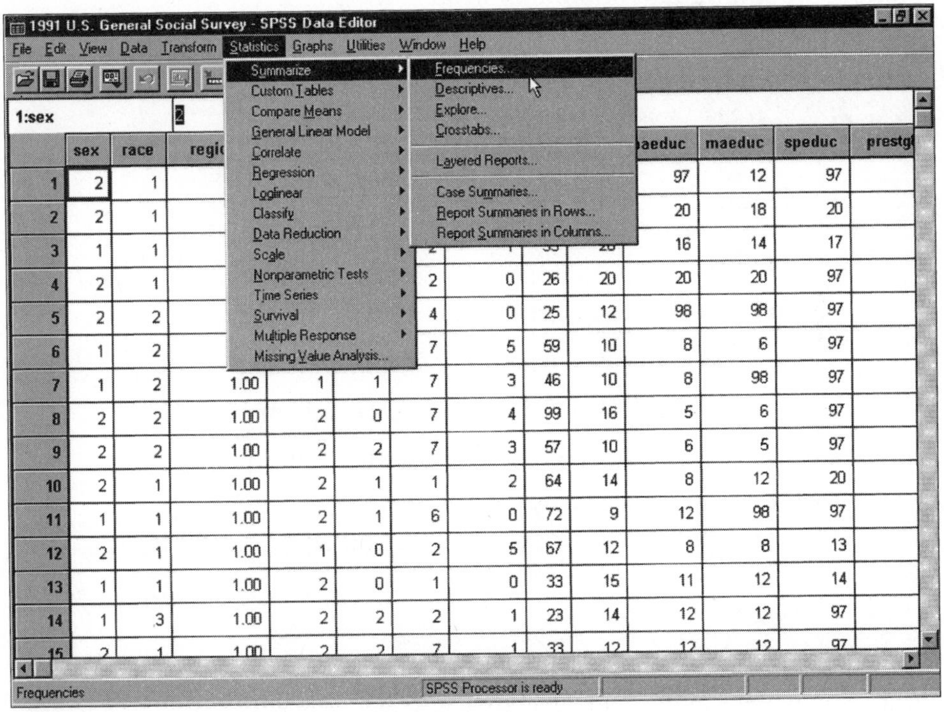

FIGURE 2.1   Choosing the Frequencies Procedure

the Windows Desktop or by pointing to the SPSS icon in the Windows Program Manager menu of program listings (i.e., Start>Programs>SPSS). After you complete this process, SPSS will load, and the active Data Editor window will appear.

Note that the Data Editor window will appear as a blank spreadsheet. One common mistake students make prior to using an SPSS statistical procedure is failing to load their datafile. Before you apply the Frequencies procedure (or any statistical procedure), you must load your data. Review Assignment 1 for directions on this process.

Figure 2.1 shows the Statistics menu with all of the options available for the analysis. Select the Summarize option from the Statistics menu by highlighting the option, pointing, and single-clicking. Once you have selected this option, SPSS will display a second set of options, including procedures used to produce frequencies, descriptive statistics, exploratory statistics, crosstabulations of data, and a variety of data summary options. (These are all procedures used to produce descriptive statistics.) Next, select the Frequencies procedure by highlighting the Frequencies option on the sub-menu, as shown in Figure 2.1 (i.e., Statistics>Summarize>Frequencies).

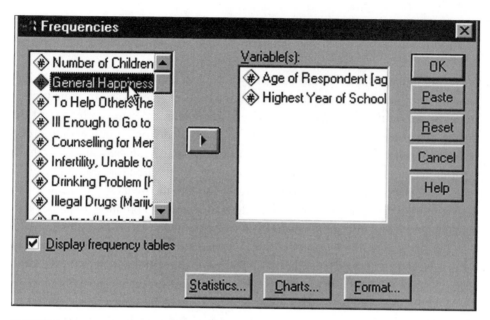

FIGURE 2.2 SPSS Frequencies Window

After you have selected Frequencies, SPSS will display another screen listing the variables in your datafile, as shown in Figure 2.2. Select the variables you wish to analyze from the variable box in the left-hand side of the window by highlighting them with the mouse and then double-clicking on them. In this example, the variables Age of Respondent (age) and Highest Year of School Completed (educ) were selected. Once you highlight and double-click on a variable, SPSS transfers it to the right-hand box, as shown in Figure 2.2. Note that variables listed in the variable box are listed by their variable labels. The variables can also be listed in the variable box by their variable names (i.e., age and educ). You can shift between these two types of listings by selecting Edit>Options and changing the preference settings. However, you should consult with your instructor before changing these settings.

To produce frequency distributions, you must point and click on the Display frequency tables box. After you point and click, a checkmark will appear in the box, and SPSS will produce frequency distributions for the variable(s) chosen. If you do not want to produce frequency distributions, pointing and clicking on the box will remove the checkmark, and SPSS will not produce frequency distributions.

Functions accessed through the Frequencies window allow you to produce a number of descriptive statistics, including measures of central tendency and graphs. Note that on this screen, you can request a chart using the Charts button.

SPSS has powerful graphics capabilities that allow you to present data in graphical form in a number of ways. (Assignment 3 explains in detail how to use this feature.)

Although not shown in this section, you can click on the Format button to format the production of frequency distributions. Researchers vary in their preferences related to the compilation of frequency distributions. Some prefer to sort the listing of frequencies in ascending order, whereas others prefer descending order.

When producing a frequency distribution with many values, you may want to restrict the number of categories appearing in the distribution for ease of presentation. You can also have SPSS limit the presentation of the frequency distribution to one page. The Frequencies Format procedure allows you to produce frequency distributions in many different formats. You can experiment with your options.

By clicking on the Statistics button, you can have SPSS produce measures of central tendency, dispersion, and the shape of the distribution. After you click the Statistics button, SPSS will produce a checklist of measures that can be obtained on each of the variables you choose to analyze. Choose measures that capture the characteristics of your data; the simple frequency distribution and measures of central tendency are primary indicators of the properties inherent to distributions.

As shown in Figure 2.3, the researcher selected a listing of the quartiles, three measures of central tendency, skewness, and several measures of dispersion. Depending on your instructor's directions, you may choose the same measures for your assignment. In describing the results, remember to select appropriate indicators to describe your variables.

After choosing the appropriate indicators, you must click on the Continue button to return to the Variable Selection menu. When the Frequencies window reappears, select the OK button. SPSS will then perform the statistical calculations on your data. Make sure that the box at the bottom of the left-hand column is checked, so that you can obtain a frequency distribution for the variables you have chosen. When the SPSS status bar indicates that the SPSS Processor is ready, your results will appear in the SPSS Viewer window.

ON YOUR OWN

You now know how to view and print the output from the SPSS Frequencies procedure. To complete the task, do the following:

1. Examine the information presented in SPSS output, focusing on the frequency distribution and measures of central tendency, dispersion, and distribution shape.

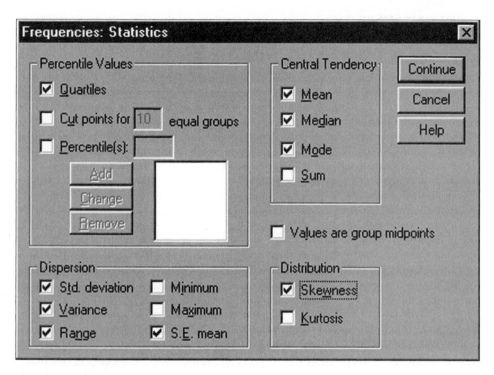

FIGURE 2.3 Frequencies: Statistics Window

2. In a brief paragraph, describe the characteristics of each of the variables you have chosen. That is, describe the characteristics of your data using the SPSS output. The best way to accomplish this is simply by pointing out interesting characteristics about the distributions of your variables. Do not simply report the values and percentages given in the SPSS output; record your own analysis of why these values and percentages are reported (e.g., Why does variable A have a mean of 40.41? or Why is the median for variable A greater than the mean?). This requires that you study the distributions and measures of central tendency and variance to detect interesting characteristics about the data. In anticipation of describing your data, review the SPSS output shown in Figure 1.11 in Assignment 1. The SPSS Viewer window shown in the figure contains information produced by the SPSS Frequencies procedure.

ASSIGNMENT 3

Presenting Data in Graphic Form

OBJECTIVES

1. To run the Chart feature in SPSS

2. To obtain a printout of an SPSS graph

3. To describe the meaning of an SPSS graph

In this assignment, you will learn how to interpret and produce a graph in SPSS. The task is not a difficult one. You will start where you ended in Assignment 2.

PRODUCING GRAPHS

When choosing the type of graph to produce, remember to select a graph that is appropriate for the scale of measure used for the variable(s) you wish to graph. Bar graphs are used to display data measured with nominal scales of measurement. Histograms are used to display variables measured using interval or ratio scales of measure. Histograms are also used to display data from continuous variables.

To produce the graph, you will first need to choose the Statistics> Summarize>Frequencies>Charts option from the Frequencies window, as shown in Assignment 2. After you click on the Charts button, SPSS will produce the Frequencies: Charts screen, as shown in Figure 3.1. The Chart window allows you to pick either a bar chart, pie chart, or histogram. If you point and click on either the bar chart or pie chart, the Chart Values area of the Frequencies: Charts window will brighten, allowing you to choose to display either frequencies or percentages. If you choose to produce a histogram, SPSS lets you display the normal curve with the histogram by pointing and clicking on the With normal curve box. Proceed with the production of the chart by clicking on the Continue button.

After you click on Continue, SPSS will begin to return to the main Frequencies screen, as illustrated in Assignment 2. After you click on the OK button, SPSS will produce the chart you requested.

After you click on the OK button in the Frequencies window, the chart or histogram will appear with your Frequencies output in the SPSS Viewer window.

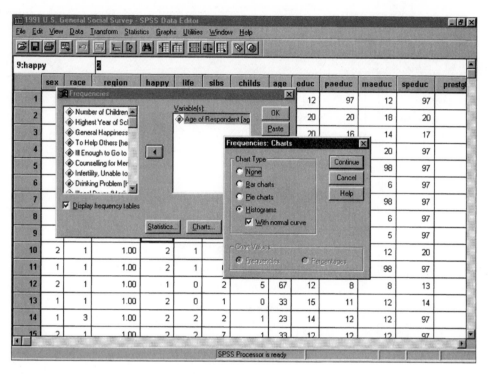

FIGURE 3.1   Using the Frequencies: Charts Window

After you point and click on the named graphics output as it appears in the left-hand pane of the SPSS Viewer window, the graphics you chose to produce will appear in the right-hand pane. Shown as Figure 3.2, this screen displays the chart that you requested. If you made charts for more than one variable, you can use the arrows that appear in the scrollbars on the right-hand side to position the graphic for viewing. For histograms, SPSS also displays some of the statistics for each variable, such as the standard deviation, the mean, and the number of cases included in the variable. If you choose to display the normal curve, it will be interposed on the graphical display of the distribution.

You should pay particular attention to how the distribution of your chosen variable conforms to the normal distribution. As shown in Figure 3.2, the variable chosen for this example does not conform to the normal distribution, having a positively skewed distribution.

Your final task in this assignment is to obtain a printout of the chart. You will print the graph from the SPSS Viewer window as shown in Assignment 1. SPSS also allows you to export the graph for insertion in other applications. After you point and click on Export, the Export Output window will appear, as shown in

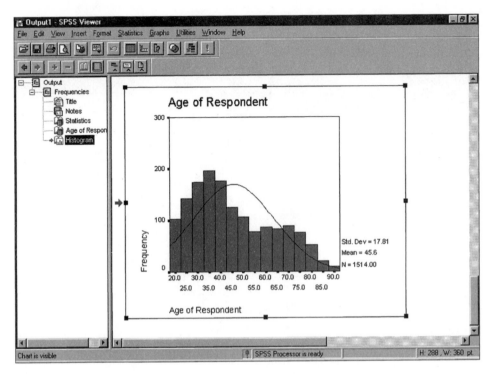

FIGURE 3.2   Displaying Graphical Output in the SPSS Viewer Window

Figure 3.3. This window allows you to choose among a number of exportable graphical file formats for use in other applications. The Export Output window also provides options for adjusting the quality of the output. You can access these options by pointing and clicking on the Options button. By pointing and clicking on the Chart Size button, you can access options for sizing the chart to fit your needs.

If you choose to print your output using the SPSS Viewer, the computer may take some time to perform this task. Graphical images are memory intensive and require time to load into the printer. In such cases, the computer and printer may appear inactive, and you may need to wait for the image to be processed and sent to the printer.

ON YOUR OWN

You are now ready to create your own graphs. To complete the exercise, do the following:

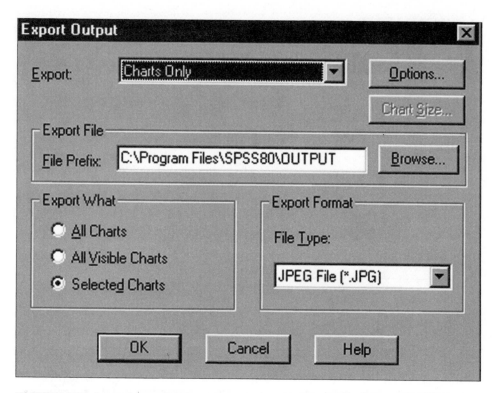

FIGURE 3.3   Export Output Window

1.   Select at least one variable from your data to graph.

2.   Obtain a printout of the graph.

3.   Describe each variable you select in a short paragraph. Specifically, describe the shape of the distribution, the skewness, and the relationship of the measures of central tendency to the shape of the distribution. Also describe the manner in which the data are dispersed. You need to think of the distributions in spatial terms. Be observant and creative in your descriptions!

ASSIGNMENT 4

Testing Research Hypotheses for Two Independent Samples

OBJECTIVES

1. To formulate research questions focusing on differences between two independent populations

2. To use the Independent-Samples T Test procedure to test the hypotheses

3. To summarize the results using output from the Independent-Samples T Test procedure

Researchers often compare different populations. To do these types of comparisons, you must utilize the appropriate statistical tests to test hypotheses about the different populations. For purposes of comparing populations on a dependent variable measured using an interval or ratio scale of measurement, the independent-samples *t* test is often the appropriate statistical test.

Prior to comparing populations, however, you must specify the comparisons to be completed. To assist in this process, you must compose research questions to guide the process of hypotheses generation and testing. Research questions are precisely worded queries about what you want to discover by comparing the populations.

For example, suppose you are looking at the education differences between men and women and want to compare the educational attainment of men and women. Implicit in this comparison is a research question, which can be formally stated as, "Does the educational attainment of men and women differ?"

Based on your knowledge of the literature and personal observation, you probably have a hunch about the gender differences in marriage age. Based on the way the research question is posed, you will choose the appropriate statistical test. In this example, the research question implies a comparison of males and females. The appropriate test for such a comparison is the independent-samples *t* test.

To properly evaluate the question, you must state these beliefs in the form of testable hypotheses prior to actually doing the independent-samples t test. (Refer to your textbook for more about hypothesis testing.) After stating your hypotheses, you will be ready to actually test the hypotheses using the independent-samples *t* test.

In this example, you will test the hypotheses using data from the 1991 General Social Survey (GSS). (This survey is a random sample of the individuals living in the United States over the age of 17. The survey is completed annually by the National Opinion Research Center at the University of Chicago and is used to track social trends.)

PERFORMING THE Independent-Samples T Test PROCEDURE

To complete the Independent-Samples T Test procedure, first click on the Statistics pull-down menu, as shown in Figure 4.1. Then click on the Compare Means option. Another sub-menu will appear listing several procedures by which to compare means, including the one-sample *t* test, independent-samples *t* test, paired-samples *t* test, and one-way ANOVA. In this assignment, you will choose the Independent-Samples T Test procedure from this list by pointing and clicking on that procedure (i.e., Statistics>Compare Means>Independent-Samples T Test). Note that SPSS uses a capital "T" as the symbol for the *t* statistic in the name of the procedure. This test is referred to in most statistical contexts as a *t* test. In this discussion, the capital "T" notation will be used only when specifically naming an SPSS procedure.

PICKING YOUR TEST AND GROUPING VARIABLES

After you choose the Independent-Samples T Test procedure, SPSS will produce a screen that lists the variables in the datafile. You will choose your variables from this list. You will need to choose two things: your test variable (dependent variable(s)) and your grouping variable (independent variable). The test variable is that variable or measure on which you want to perform the *t* test in order to test your hypotheses. The grouping variable defines the two independent samples you want to compare using the Independent-Samples T Test procedure.

In the example used in this assignment, you are interested in comparing the educational attainment of men and women. To accomplish this, choose sex from the list and insert it into the Grouping Variable box, as shown in Figure 4.2. For the test variable, you insert the Highest Year School Completed (educ) variable into the Test Variable box.

For this assignment, you will pick your own test variables unless otherwise specified by your instructor. You must remember to use variables measured using the appropriate scale of measurement. You should pick variables measured in

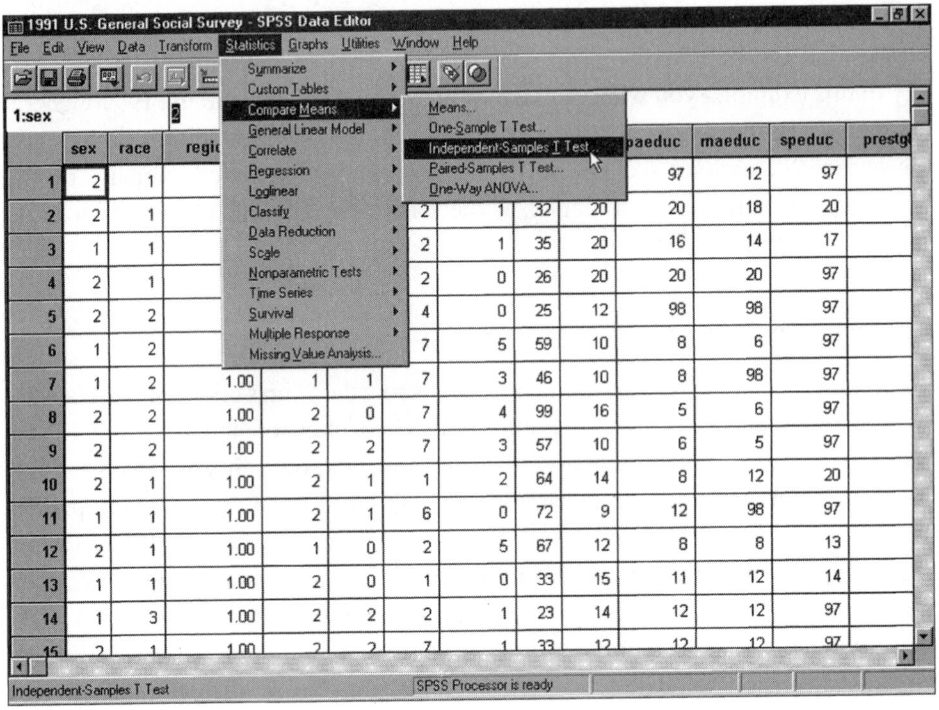

FIGURE 4.1   Accessing the Independent-Samples T Test Procedure

either interval or ratio scales of measure. The independent-samples *t* test is not an appropriate procedure to use with other scales of measure.

When you insert the grouping variable into the box, SPSS will prompt you to define the values of the grouping variable (i.e., the two question marks). You need to point and click on the Define Groups button. Another screen will appear allowing you to define the variables, as shown in Figure 4.3. In the GSS example, the sex variable is defined with two values: 1 for men and 2 for women. As you can see in Figure 4.3, the value associated with group 1 is "1" and with group 2 is "2." These are the values for males and females in the GSS dataset, respectively. Once you have defined the groups, point and click on the Continue button, and you will return to the screen shown in Figure 4.2.

When you complete the selection process, return to the Independent-Samples T Test procedure screen and click on OK to execute the procedure. SPSS will produce the results of the analysis in the SPSS Viewer window. To print the results from the Independent-Samples T Test procedure, invoke the Printing procedure with the SPSS Viewer window on top. Review how to print SPSS output from Assignment 1 prior to printing the SPSS Viewer window.

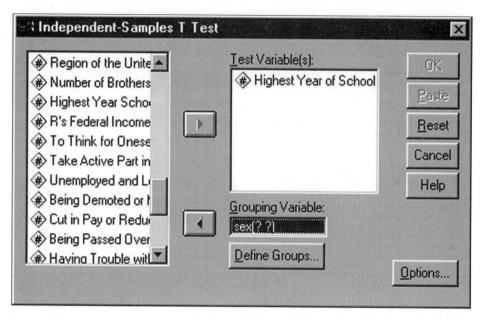

FIGURE 4.2 Choosing the Test and Grouping Variables

INTERPRETING THE OUTPUT

The example used in this assignment provides an illustration for use in the interpretation of results from the Independent-Samples T Test procedure. Note that interpretation of this type of *t* test from SPSS output is a two-stage process.

The first stage involves assessing the homogeneity of variance between the populations. To use the independent-samples *t* test to test hypotheses, a number of assumptions about the populations being compared must be made. When using this form of the independent-samples *t* test, the researcher assumes that the variance in the populations being compared is the same. The Independent-Samples T Test procedure tests this assumption by using Levene's Test for Equality of Variances, as shown in Figure 4.4. This test is based on the *F* statistic (something you will learn more about in later assignments). SPSS computes both an *F* value and *p* value. The *F* value is the actual value computed for the *F* statistic. The *p* value is the calculated probability for making a Type I error (sometimes referred to as the obtained alpha level). The *p* value allows you to determine whether the populations have equal variances. If the *p* value is less than .05 ($p < .05$), the Levene's test indicates that the variances between the populations are not equal. But if the *p* value is greater than .05, the population variances are very close.

Based on the results obtained in the first stage of the interpretation process, you can now evaluate the hypotheses tested using the independent-samples *t* test.

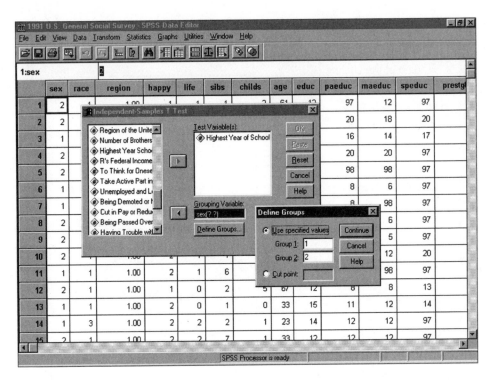

FIGURE 4.3   Defining the Groups

The results of the *t* test are found on the printout (and in the SPSS Viewer display as shown in Figure 4.4) as a table summarizing the t-test for Equality of Means. Note that the table contains two rows of results. One row of results is labeled as Equal Variances Assumed and the other row as Equal Variances Not Assumed. If the Levene's test indicates that the variances of the two populations are about the same, you should use the results as indicated in the row where variances are assumed equal. If the Levene's test indicates unequal population variances, you should use the results as indicated in the row where equal variances are not assumed.

In the example used in this assignment and illustrated in Figure 4.4, the Levene's test indicates that equal variances are not assumed. In this case, you should use the results indicated in the Equal Variances Not Assumed row. Notice that these results are slightly different from those indicated in the other row. In the event of unequal variances, SPSS mathematically adjusts the results of the *t* test to account for the inequality evidenced in the two populations.

Once you determine which row of results to use, you can then directly evaluate the results of the Independent-Samples T Test procedure. Note that SPSS

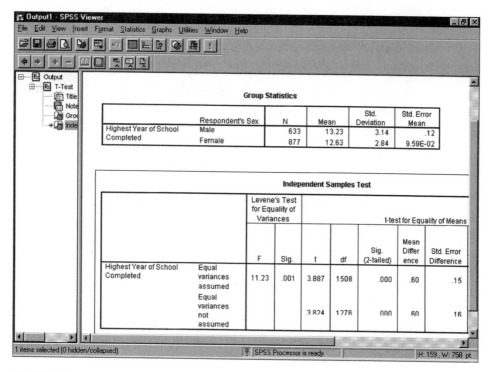

FIGURE 4.4 SPSS Output for the Independent-Samples T Test

calculates a *t* value and provides the degrees of freedom (df) on the printout. These are the same values you would calculate manually using the GSS data. SPSS also calculates a Sig. (2-tailed) value. This value is the actual probability of making a Type I error. If this value is less than the specified alpha level (usually $p = .05$ or $p = .01$) used in testing the set of hypotheses, you should "reject" the null hypothesis. By rejecting the null hypothesis, you would conclude that the two populations are different. On the other hand, values greater than the specified alpha level require that you "fail to reject" the null hypothesis. In this case, you would conclude that insufficient evidence exists to suggest that the two populations are different.

In the example used in this assignment, SPSS indicates that the Sig. (2-tailed) value is less than .05, a normally specified alpha level. Consequently, you can conclude that a statistically significant difference exists between educational attainment of men and women. By doing so, you are rejecting the null hypothesis that states that no difference exists between men and women in terms of their educational attainment. The means indicated that the average educational attainment of men is greater than that of women.

ON YOUR OWN

You are now ready to test some hypotheses of your own using the Independent-Samples T Test. To complete this task, do the following:

1. State your research question based on the two variables you choose or your instructor directs you to use.

2. State your hypotheses for use in comparing two independent samples.

3. Test your hypotheses using the Independent-Samples T Test procedure.

4. Write a one- or two-sentence conclusion detailing the results and the meaning of your hypothesis test in terms of the dependent and independent variables.

ASSIGNMENT 5

Testing Research Hypotheses About Two Related Samples

OBJECTIVES

1. To devise questions about differences between two related populations

2. To formulate hypotheses based on the research questions

3. To use the Paired-Samples T Test procedure to test the stated hypotheses

4. To use output from the Paired-Samples T Test procedure to summarize and interpret the results of the hypothesis test

---

Use Anxiety 2

The Paired-Samples T Test procedure is used to evaluate whether the means of two related populations are different. What relationship between the populations is examined depends on what research question is being asked. A common research question is, "After participants in a study receive a treatment, will they behave very differently than they did prior to the treatment?" Because this question calls for the measurement of the responses of the same group of participants before treatment and after treatment, the research design can be labeled as a repeated-measures design, a pre-test, post-test design, or a before-and-after design.

Note that SPSS uses a capital "T" as the symbol for the t statistic in the name of this procedure—Paired-Samples T Test. As was explained in Assignment 4, this is not standard practice. In the discussion that follows, the capital "T" notation will be used only when specifically naming the SPSS Paired-Samples T Test procedure. Otherwise, a lowercase italicized t will be used as the symbol for the t statistic.

THE RESEARCH QUESTION AND DESIGN

The Repeated-Measures Design

An example of a repeated-measures study is one that asks, "Does a memory-enhancing drug have an effect on the ability of a group of Alzheimer's patients to memorize a list of words?" Prior to the administration of the drug, memory for the list of words is tested. Following the drug treatment, the memory ability of each patient is measured again. In the *t* test analysis, the pre-treatment score and the post-treatment score are compared for each patient.

The Matched-Groups Design

The paired-samples *t* test is also used when the research question involves differences between two separate groups of participants but the researcher wants to ensure that the two groups are evenly matched before the study begins. The design used to answer this research question is called the matched-groups design. In this design, the researcher matches participants on a variable related to the dependent variable to ensure that relevant characteristics of one group correspond to the other group prior to treatment.

An example of a research question that leads to this kind of design is, "Would a group of students that had taken a training program do better on the Graduate Record Examination (GRE) than another group that had not?" If, by chance, one group of students starts out with considerably less academic ability than the other, the study could be seriously biased. To ensure that the bias is minimized, the researcher first determines the grade-point average (GPA) of each member of a sample of students and then ranks them according to those averages. The two highest-ranking students are then randomly assigned, one to the control group and one to the treatment group. Each successive pair of students in the ranking is then assigned in the same way. This ensures that the distribution of academic ability (as measured by the student's GPA) is quite similar in both groups.

Following the matching procedure, the treatment group is then given training while the control group gets none. Both groups then take the GRE. The scores of the members of each matched pair are compared in the *t* test analysis as if they had been produced by the same person.

THE HYPOTHESES

For both of the research questions, the null hypothesis is that the means of the populations represented by the treatment and control groups are equal (two-tailed test) or that they differ in a direction other than had been predicted (one-tailed test). If the null hypothesis can be rejected, then the alternative or research hypothesis can be supported. As in the independent-samples *t* test, the data to be analyzed must be measured on an interval or ratio scale.

The following procedure uses a dataset related to the drug treatment for patients with Alzheimer's disease in the example mentioned previously. The independent variable is the drug treatment status of the Alzheimer's patient (pre-

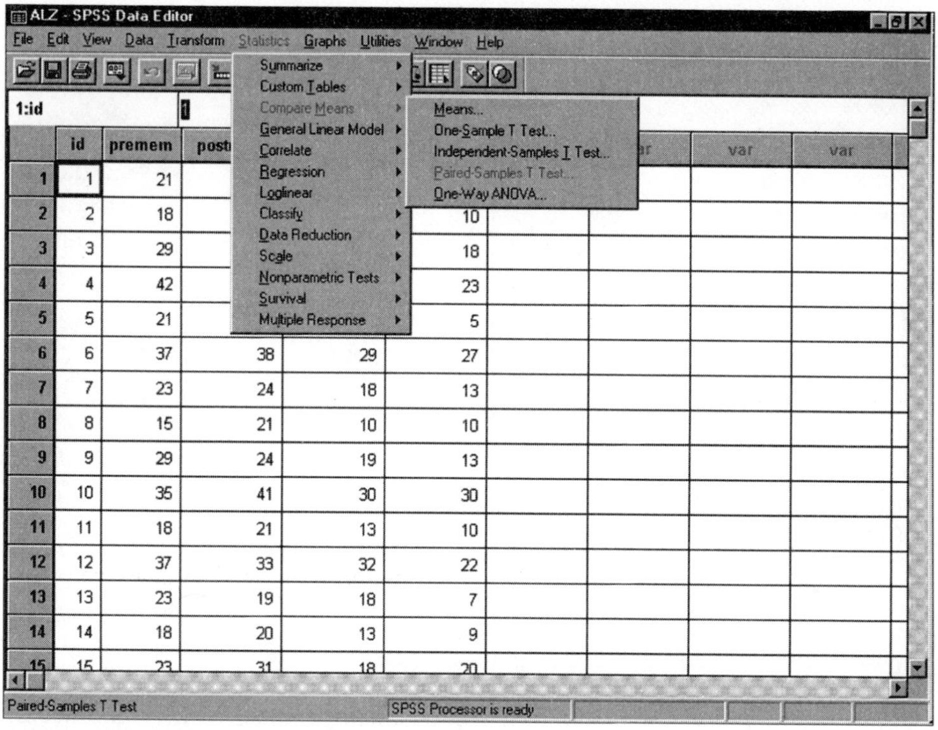

FIGURE 5.1 Selecting the Paired-Samples T Test Procedure

treatment or post-treatment). The dependent variable is number of words recalled from 100 words presented during a memory test.

EXECUTING THE Paired-Samples T Test PROCEDURE

To perform the Paired-Samples T Test procedure, you must first click on the Statistics pull-down menu. Then, from the Statistics menu, click on the Compare Means option. You are then presented with a final menu listing five statistical procedures used to compare means, as shown in Figure 5.1. Choose the Paired-Samples T Test option from this menu (i.e., Statistics>Compare Means>Paired-Samples T Test).

When you choose the Paired-Samples T Test option, SPSS advances to a screen containing a box that lists the variables in the datafile. Because every participant contributes memory data for both treatment conditions, a grouping variable is not used. Instead, data for both measures of memory ability are entered under two different variable names. In this example, as Figure 5.2 shows, the measures of memory test performance from the pre-treatment and post-treatment conditions are

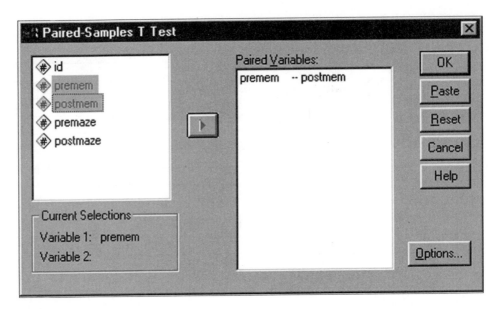

FIGURE 5.2   Selecting the Paired Variables

represented by the variables premem and postmem, respectively. Click once on each of these two related variables and then move them into the box labeled Paired Variables by clicking on the arrow button between the two boxes. Run the procedure by clicking the OK button.

INTERPRETING THE OUTPUT

SPSS will output the results of the analysis after processing the data via the SPSS Viewer, as shown in Figure 5.3. The first two tables provided in the output for the analysis contain descriptive statistics for each of the variables. The first table (not shown) provides the mean, standard deviation, and standard error for both variables. The table labeled Paired Samples Correlations presents the bivariate correlation between the two variables and its statistical significance. It is important to look at this correlation because if it is not significant (Sig. > .05), then questions may be raised about the relationship between the two variables and/or the validity of the experimental design. The correlation shown in this example is relatively high ($r = .820$) and is significant at $p < .001$ (SPSS provides significance levels to only three decimal places; anything less than that is printed as .000).

The Paired Samples Test table reflects the analysis of the difference between the two variables. The most important elements of this group are the t test statistic (t),

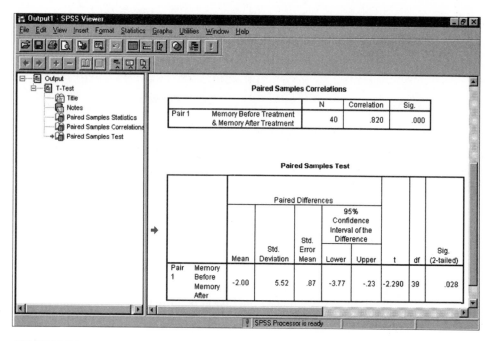

FIGURE 5.3 Output for the Drug/Alzheimer's Example

the degrees of freedom (df), and the two-tailed significance level (Sig. (2-tailed)), which appear in the last three columns of the table. These statistics provide the test of the null hypothesis. The t value of -2.290 in this example is negative simply because the mean of the premem scores is smaller than the mean of the postmem scores. The degrees of freedom are equal to the number of pairs of memory test scores minus one ($40 - 1 = 39$).

The two-tailed significance level for this analysis directly provides the probability for making an error in judgment (Type I error) if you choose to say there is a difference between the populations represented by the two variables. The criterion value (usually $p = .05$ or $p = .01$) for making such errors is compared to the value provided by the t test. If the value obtained from the analysis is less than the criterion value you chose before the study began, then you may reject the null hypothesis and infer that the means of two populations represented by your variables are different.

For the drug and Alzheimer's example, a criterion value for making an alpha error of $p = .05$ and a two-tailed hypothesis are assumed. The two-tailed probability value obtained from the analysis (Sig. = .028) is less than the criterion value. If you have a one-tailed hypothesis, divide the two-tailed significance level in half

$(.028 \div 2 = .014)$ and make the comparison with your criterion value. In either case, you would be correct to reject the null hypothesis and support the notion that the drug significantly changed the memory of Alzheimer's patients.

ON YOUR OWN

You are now familiar with the Paired-Samples T Test procedure to examine pairs of related variables. Using your own data or a dataset provided by your instructor, analyze the effect of the independent variable on the dependent variable. To complete this task, do the following:

1. Write out (in words) the null hypothesis and an alternate hypothesis for this analysis. Specify whether it is a one-tailed or two-tailed hypothesis.

2. Perform the analysis using the Paired-Samples T Test procedure, and print the output.

3. Write a one- or two-sentence conclusion detailing the results and the meaning of your hypothesis test in terms of the independent and dependent variables.

look at means

ASSIGNMENT 6

Comparing Independent Samples with One-Way ANOVA

OBJECTIVES

1. To formulate a research question about the differences between more than two groups

2. To test a hypothesis about multiple groups using the SPSS One-Way ANOVA procedure

3. To provide an interpretation of the results of the One-Way ANOVA procedure

4. To provide an interpretation of the Scheffé and Tukey post hoc tests

---

Many analytic scenarios require the researcher to compare more than two populations or treatment conditions. Suppose you were a biomedical researcher studying the effects of new pharmaceuticals on headaches. You might want to compare the effectiveness of different types of drugs on headache relief. Similarly, you might want to assess the differences among individuals provided varied dosages of a new drug.

Making simple comparisons between two populations or treatment conditions is not problematic, because *t* tests provide an appropriate statistical test for such comparisons. Making comparisons of multiple treatments or populations, however, complicates the process. You would need to do multiple *t* tests to complete all of the needed comparisons. The One-Way ANOVA statistic provides a means of making statistical comparisons across two or more groups and alleviates the need to conduct multiple *t* tests. The SPSS One-Way ANOVA procedure performs such comparisons across multiple populations or treatment conditions.

PERFORMING THE One-Way ANOVA PROCEDURE

Suppose you are a cardiologist who is studying a sample of heart patients. One of the dependent variables being used in the study is the cholesterol count of the patients. A research question you might ask is, "How does the cholesterol level of the patients compare across the young, middle-age, and older groups?"

To answer this question, you would divide patients into three age-defined groups: those under 35 years of age (young), those between 36 and 50 years old (middle age), and those over 50 (older). You would then examine the mean cholesterol levels for each group of patients.

Given the way the research question is phrased and the fact that you have more than two groups to compare, the One-Way ANOVA is the appropriate statistical test for this analytic scenario. To conduct the test, you need to load your data into SPSS and access the One-Way ANOVA procedure.

As shown in Figure 6.1, you first move the mouse to the Statistics pull-down menu from the list of statistical procedures. Select the Compare Means procedure. After you highlight Compare Means, a sub-menu will appear containing different procedures used to compare means. Highlight the One-Way ANOVA procedure from the list. Once you have highlighted the procedure, SPSS will generate the One-Way ANOVA window.

CHOOSING AND DEFINING YOUR VARIABLES

The variables in your datafile will appear in the left-hand box of the One-Way ANOVA window, as shown in Figure 6.2. Choose your dependent variable by highlighting it and clicking on the arrow toggle pointing at the Dependent List box. In this example, you have chosen the variable cholcnt (cholesterol level). You have also chosen the agegr (age group) variable into the Factor box as your grouping variable.

PERFORMING POST HOC TESTS

You can choose to have SPSS calculate descriptive statistics, post hoc multiple comparisons, and homogeneity-of-variance tests by clicking on the Post Hoc and Options buttons in the main One-Way ANOVA windows. First, click on the Post Hoc button to access the Post Hoc Multiple Comparisons window, as shown in Figure 6.3. SPSS allows you to select a variety of post hoc tests for assessing the differences between individual pairs of means. Post hoc tests are similar to t tests in that they test the differences between pairs of sample means. (Remember that the ANOVA procedure only detects differences between any pair of sample means.) In this example, you have selected two post hoc tests: the Tukey's Honestly Significant Difference test and the Scheffé test. You will obtain SPSS output on both of these tests.

Return to the One-Way ANOVA window and click on the Options button. SPSS will produce the Options window, as shown in Figure 6.4. Click on the Descriptive

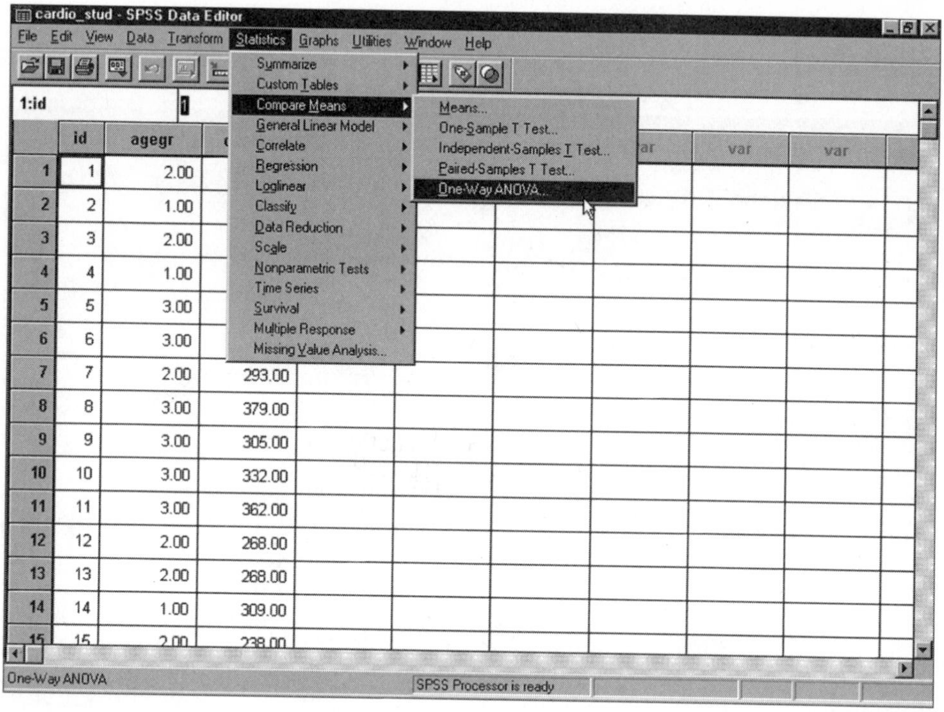

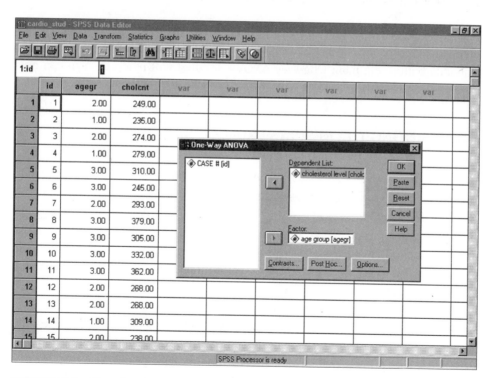

FIGURE 6.1 Choosing the One-Way ANOVA Procedure

FIGURE 6.2 Choosing the Dependent and Factor Variables

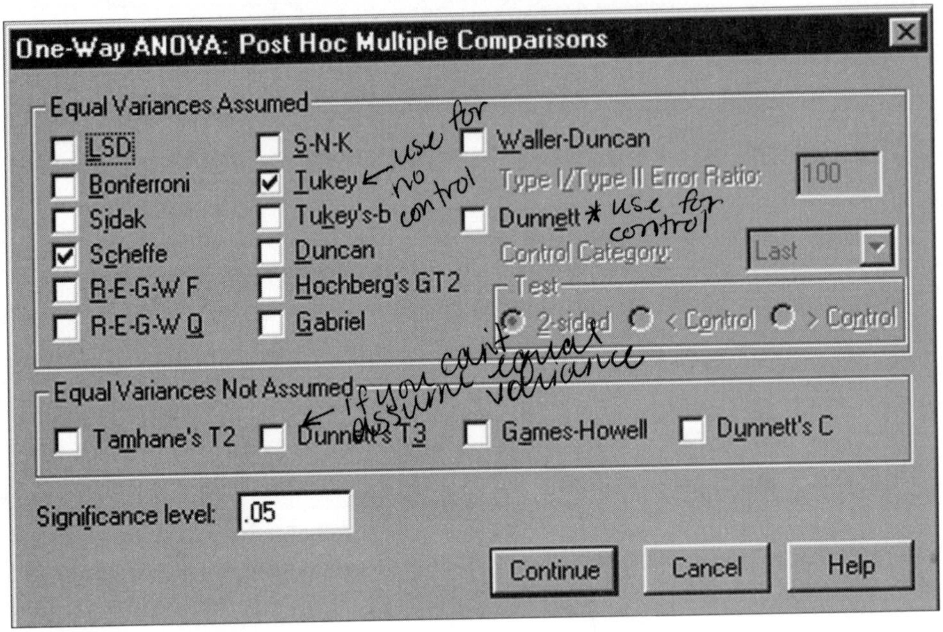

FIGURE 6.3   One-Way ANOVA: Post Hoc Multiple Comparisons

box and the Homogeneity-of-variance box for a Levene's test. After you click on the Continue button, the main One-Way ANOVA window will reappear. You can now instruct SPSS to compute the One-Way ANOVA by clicking on the OK button.

INTERPRETING THE RESULTS FROM
THE One-Way ANOVA PROCEDURE

After you run the One-Way ANOVA procedure, the SPSS Viewer window (shown in Figures 6.5 and 6.6) presents the results. Figure 6.5 shows the descriptive statistics calculated by the One-Way ANOVA procedure. These statistics include the number of observations in each age group, the mean cholesterol count for each age group, and the standard deviations and errors for each group. If you shift the output pane to the right by using the right arrow scroll button, you will find the confidence intervals calculated by the procedure as well.

The One-Way ANOVA procedure also calculates a Test of Homogeneity of Variances. As with the Independent-Samples T Test procedure, SPSS uses the Levene statistic for the calculation of this test. In this example, the homogeneity of variances assumption is met as indicated by the Sig. value greater than .05.

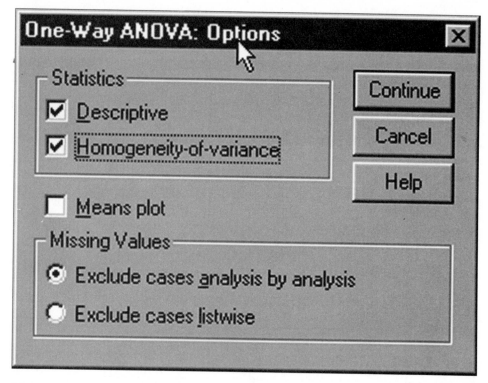

FIGURE 6.4   Choosing One-Way ANOVA Options

In Figure 6.5, SPSS provides information on the One-Way ANOVA statistic by summarizing the results of the test in the concise ANOVA table. The table has calculations for the Between Groups, Within Groups, and Total Sum of Squares. The ANOVA table also provides calculations of the between- and within-groups Mean Squares. The Mean Squares data are used to calculate the F statistic. SPSS presents the calculation of the F statistic as the F. SPSS also calculates the probability of making a Type I error as the Sig.

Figure 6.5 provides the results of your comparisons of three age groups relative to their cholesterol levels. The Sig. value indicates that the likelihood of committing a Type I error is .0000 ($p < .0001$). Assuming you are testing the hypothesis at a criterion level (alpha level) of $p = .01$, you can reject the null hypothesis because $p < .0001$ is less than $p = .01$.

INTERPRETING THE POST HOC TESTS

By examining the group means shown as descriptive statistics at the top of Figure 6.5, you can see differences between the groups being compared in the study. However, the results from the One-Way ANOVA procedure do not indicate which of

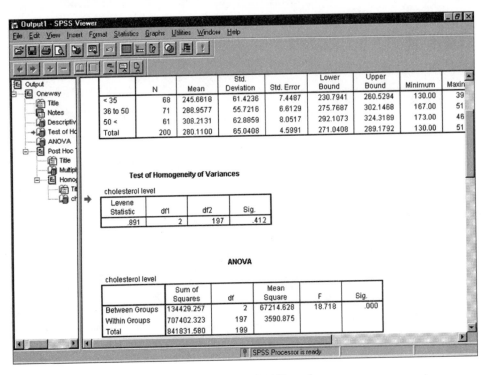

FIGURE 6.5   SPSS Output for the One-Way ANOVA Procedure

these group means have statistically significant differences between them. To evaluate which groups differ from one another, you must turn to the results of the post hoc tests as calculated by SPSS.

Figure 6.6 shows the results from both the Tukey and the Scheffé post hoc tests for each pair of groups being compared. Note the results of the Tukey test. The first and second rows of output show the results of the test comparing the average cholesterol counts between the "age 35 or younger" group and both the "36- to 50-year-old" and the "older than age 50" groups. In the first comparison, between those "35 or younger" and the "36- to 50-year-old" groups, the mean difference was –43.296. The asterisk (*) displayed with the mean difference indicates that a statistically significant difference in cholesterol counts exist between the two age groups. Similarly, there is a difference between the "age 35 or younger" and the "older than age 50" groups. The second row in the display indicates that these two groups have a mean difference of –62.5514. Again, the asterisk (*) indicates that a statistically significant difference relative to the average cholesterol count exists between the two age groups. The results of the Scheffé post hoc test are interpreted in the same manner.

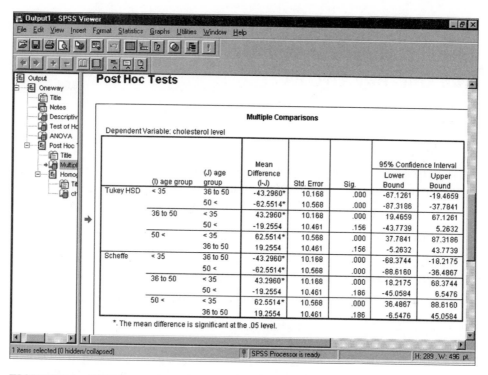

FIGURE 6.6   SPSS Output for the Tukey and Scheffé Post Hoc Tests

ON YOUR OWN

You are now ready to use the One-Way ANOVA procedure to evaluate the differences between multiple groups. To complete this task, do the following:

1.   State your research question based on two of the variables you choose or your instructor directs you to use.

2.   Test your hypotheses using the One-Way ANOVA procedure.

3.   Test between-group differences using a post hoc test.

4.   Summarize the findings as reported by both the ANOVA and the post hoc tests in paragraph form. Describe your results in terms of the independent and dependent variables.

ASSIGNMENT 7

Comparing Related Samples with One-Way ANOVA

OBJECTIVES

1. To devise research questions about differences among three or more populations that are related along the same variable

2. To formulate hypotheses based on the research questions

3. To use SPSS and the GLM - Repeated Measures procedure to test the stated hypotheses

4. To use output from the GLM - Repeated Measures procedure to summarize and interpret the results of the hypothesis test

---

SPSS presents one-way repeated-measures ANOVA as a subset of the General Linear Model (GLM) option in the Statistics menu. To use the GLM - Repeated Measures procedure, you or your computer lab must have installed the SPSS for Windows Advanced Statistics option.

Like the paired-samples *t* test, repeated-measures ANOVA is used to evaluate whether related populations are different. Unlike the paired-samples *t* test, however, repeated-measures ANOVA can be used to examine the relationship among more than two related populations. The nature of the relationship depends on what research questions are asked and what research designs are used to answer them. Repeated-measures ANOVA can be used to analyze results from both repeated-measures and matched-groups designs (see Assignment 5) with three or more treatments representing different levels of a single independent variable. This procedure is commonly referred to as one-way repeated-measures ANOVA.

THE RESEARCH QUESTION AND DESIGN

Suppose you observe that infants attend to pictures of human faces longer than to pictures of face-irrelevant geometric shapes. You could ask, "Does the organization of facial elements (position of eyes, nose, mouth, etc.) have an effect on the ability of infants to perceive human faces?" A simple one-way repeated-measures research design might use three different conditions to study this question. A control or baseline condition (Condition A) would involve exposing the infants to a blank oval. In two other conditions, the infants would be exposed to the same oval, but with human eyes, nose, mouth, and ears added. In one of these conditions (Condition B), the features would be randomly placed on the oval, while in the other (Condition C), the features would be arranged in their typical facial location.

As the phrase "repeated measures" implies, each infant would be exposed to all three conditions. In each condition, the appropriate face stimulus (A, B, or C) would be placed in front of the infant and remain there until the infant looked at it. The length of time (in 0.1-second units) that each infant initially gazed at the picture before looking away would be measured. This measure of attention span would be used as the dependent variable. To control for the effects of experience and order of presentation, each infant would be randomly assigned to a different order of conditions (ABC, ACB, BAC, BCA, CAB, CBA). Because there are six possible orders of three conditions, an attempt would be made to assign an equal number of infants to each of the six orders.

THE HYPOTHESES

The null hypothesis for the research question tested with one-way repeated-measures ANOVA is that the mean attention spans of the populations represented by the three conditions (A, B, and C) are the same. The corresponding alternative hypothesis is simply that attention spans are not equal among these populations. Following the initial analysis of the simple hypotheses, planned comparisons and post hoc comparisons may be used to investigate more complex issues such as where the significant differences among the conditions might exist.

PERFORMING THE GLM - Repeated Measures PROCEDURE

The following procedure uses a dataset related to the face recognition study just described. As in the paired-measures *t* test, data for the measures of attention span are entered under different variable names. In this example, the measure of attention span from Condition A (the blank oval), Condition B (randomly arranged features), and Condition C (facial features in their typical position on the oval) are represented by the variable names oval, rand, and face, respectively.

To perform a one-way repeated-measures ANOVA, you must first click on the Statistics pull-down menu. Then, from the Statistics menu, click on the General Linear Model item, as shown in Figure 7.1. You are then presented with a final menu containing a choice of GLM procedures. Choose the GLM - Repeated Measures item in this menu. In summary, use the following path to get to the GLM - Repeated Measures procedure: Statistics>General Linear Model>GLM - Repeated Measures.

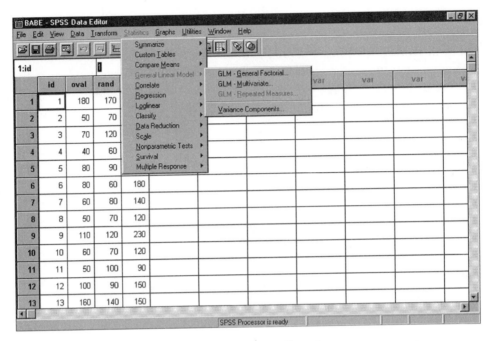

FIGURE 7.1   Selecting the GLM - Repeated Measures Procedure

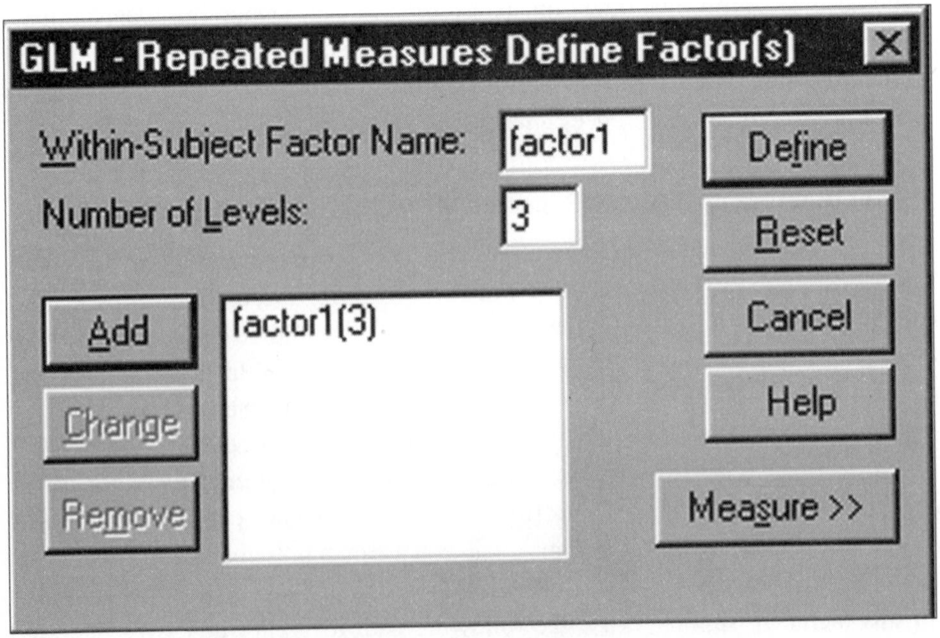

FIGURE 7.2   Indicating the Number of Within-Subject Factors

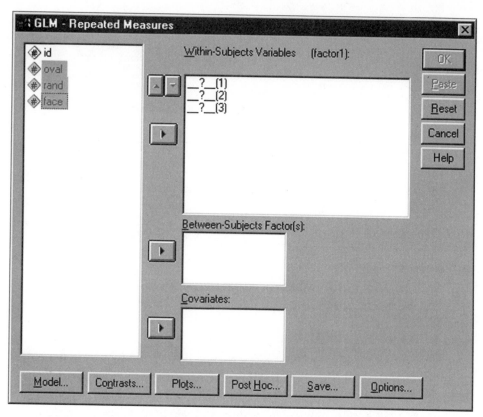

FIGURE 7.3   Selecting and Defining the Within-Subjects Variables

When you choose the GLM - Repeated Measures option, SPSS advances to a screen containing a box labeled GLM - Repeated Measures Define Factor(s), as shown in Figure 7.2. SPSS provides the variable name factor1 in the Within-Subject Factor Name text box. This variable name cannot be one you have used for your data. It is simplest to use the default name that the procedure provides (i.e., factor1). The number you provide in the Number of Levels text box should be equal to the number of repeated-measures conditions that you want to analyze. In this example, you should enter "3." Next, click on the Add button and then on the Define button. You will then see the screen labeled GLM - Repeated Measures, as shown in Figure 7.3.

In this screen, you should indicate which conditions are to be analyzed. To do this, click on oval and then on the arrow button to the left of the Within-Subjects Variables (factor1) box. This will move the oval variable into the box as the first within-subjects variable. Repeat this process for the rand and face variables. When all three variables have been defined (moved) in this way, click on the OK button to run the procedure.

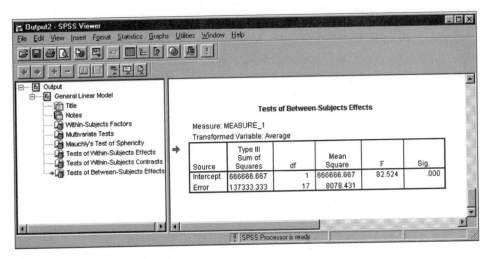

FIGURE 7.4   Testing for Between-Subjects Effects

INTERPRETING THE OUTPUT

Testing Between-Subjects Effects

Figure 7.4 shows the first group of test statistics you should look at in the output from the repeated-measures ANOVA as shown by the SPSS Viewer. This test, labeled Tests of Between-Subjects Effects, examines a special null hypothesis for the analysis. This null hypothesis states that the average of the means of the populations represented by all three variables is equal to zero. In the example used in this exercise, the experimental design allows the researcher to ignore this test. Because timing would not begin until the infants looked at the face stimulus, none of the attention times would be zero. Therefore, this special null hypothesis would be false before any data were gathered. The F value of 82.524 is significant at Sig. = .000 ($p < .001$), indicating that the null hypothesis can be rejected. However, if the dependent variable had been defined as difference scores between a baseline condition and the three attention conditions, then it would be possible for the average means for the groups to be zero, and so the test of significance for between-subjects effects would be meaningful.

Testing Sphericity

The Mauchly sphericity test shown in Figure 7.5 is used like the correlation statistic for the paired-samples t test discussed in Assignment 5. It tests another special null hypothesis concerning an assumption of sphericity that must be met in order to decide which ANOVA test should be used. Essentially, the sphericity

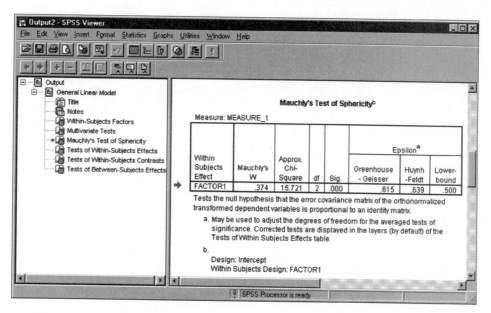

FIGURE 7.5 Testing the Sphericity Assumption

assumption is that the correlations among the attention times for the three conditions are equal. The result of the Mauchly sphericity test determines whether a univariate or a multivariate F test should be used for the one-way repeated-measures ANOVA. The chi-square statistic is used to test whether that null hypothesis should be rejected. If the chi-square statistic is not significant (not less than the criterion alpha level decided on before the experiment began, e.g., $p < .05$), then the univariate test described below should be used. If the chi-square is significant ($p < .05$), then SPSS provides two alternatives: (1) Correct the test statistic by using one of the epsilon weights (which follow the Mauchly sphericity test) to adjust degrees of freedom for the univariate test, or (2) use the multivariate
54
test. The procedure used in the application of the epsilon weights is fairly complex, so we recommend that you use one of the multivariate tests that are resistant to violations of the sphericity assumption.

The Multivariate Test

For the attention span example, the sphericity assumption has been violated (Approx. Chi-square = 15.721, Sig. = .000, $p < .001$), so you should use one of the multivariate tests shown in Figure 7.6. The most frequently used statistic is the

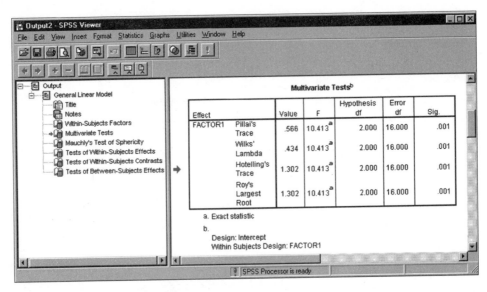

FIGURE 7.6   Multivariate F Tests for the Attention Span Example

Wilks' Lambda. In this example, the Wilks' Lambda value of 10.413 with 2 and 16 degrees of freedom is used to test the general null hypothesis that the means of the populations represented by Conditions A, B, and C are equal. The F value used to test this hypothesis is significant at Sig. = .001, indicating that you can reject the general null hypothesis and support the research hypothesis that the arrangement of the features has a significant effect on the attention span of the infants.

The Univariate Test

If the Mauchly sphericity test is not significant (Sig. > .05), then you should use the univariate test shown in Figure 7.7. The F value for Factor1 represents the test of the general null hypothesis. The F value of 14.217 with 2 and 34 degrees of freedom is significant at Sig. = .000 ($p < .001$).

Paired Comparisons

When the general null hypothesis has been rejected, it is usually of interest to ask which populations differ significantly from one another. If you decide which comparisons are to be made before the data are gathered, then they are called "planned comparisons." If you decide which groups to compare after the data are analyzed, then the comparisons are referred to as "post hoc." Unfortunately,

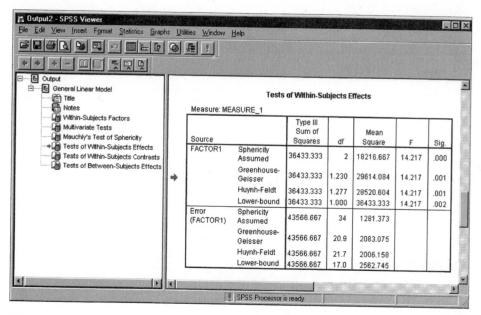

FIGURE 7.7 Univariate *F* Test for the Attention Span Example

neither planned nor post hoc comparisons are provided by the GLM - Repeated Measures procedure.

A simple way to perform both planned and post hoc comparisons is to use the paired-samples *t* test to make each comparison. In the infant attention span example used here, there are three possible comparisons: A and B, A and C, and B and C. However, the probability of making an alpha error is not unique to each comparison but is additive across all possible comparisons. In the present example, you would not be testing at the criterion alpha level of $\alpha = .05$, but at $\alpha = .15$ (i.e., $.05 + .05 + .05$).

The solution to this problem is to make a correction in the criterion alpha level. This involves simply dividing the criterion alpha level used in the general *F* test by the number of possible comparisons. In the present example, that would be $\alpha = .05 \div 3$ or $\alpha = .0167$. The criterion value of $\alpha = .0167$ is then used for making the decision to reject the null hypothesis for the paired-sample *t* test comparisons. Note that a one-tailed *t* test should be used, so the probability values obtained for the *t* tests should be divided by two before the significance of the comparison is determined.

Figure 7.8 shows the *t* tests for the three comparisons. The interpretation may be summarized as follows.

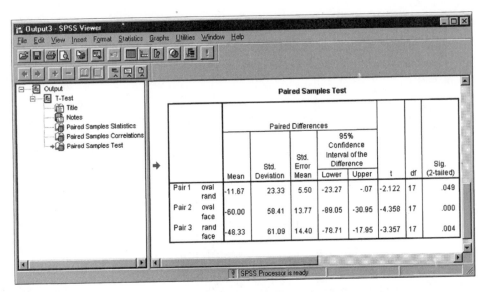

FIGURE 7.8   Post Hoc Comparison *T* Tests for the Attention Span Example

Comparison of **oval** *and* **rand**

The obtained alpha value of $p = .0245$ (Sig. $= .049 \div 2$) was not less than the criterion value, $\alpha = .0167$. This means that the *t* value of 2.122 was not large enough to reject the null hypothesis. Therefore, you could not say that infants would respond differently to the blank oval than they would to the oval with scrambled features.

Comparison of **oval** *and* **face**

The obtained alpha value of $p < .0005$ (Sig. $< .001 \div 2$) was less than the criterion value, $\alpha = .0167$. This means that the *t* value of 4.358 was large enough to reject the null hypothesis. Therefore, you could conclude that attention times for infants looking at a blank oval would be significantly less than for those looking at an oval with normally arranged facial features.

Comparison of **rand** *and* **face**

The obtained alpha value of $p < .002$ (Sig. $= .004 \div 2$) was less than the criterion value, $\alpha = .0167$. The *t* value of 3.357 was large enough to reject the null hypothesis. Therefore, you would be justified in concluding that attention times for infants looking at an oval with scrambled facial features would be significantly less than for those looking at an oval with normally arranged facial features.

General Conclusion

The comparison of attention times for oval and rand indicates that the mere presence of facial features is not sufficient to significantly change infants' attention to facelike stimuli. However, attention span is significantly increased when facial features are presented in a configuration that is typical of a human face.

ON YOUR OWN

You are now familiar with the GLM - Repeated Measures procedure to analyze three or more levels of an independent variable. Using your own data or data provided by your instructor, you are ready to run this one-way repeated-measures ANOVA. To complete this task, do the following:

1. Write out (in words) the null hypothesis and alternate hypothesis for this analysis. Is it a one- or two-tailed hypothesis?

2. Perform the analysis using the GLM - Repeated Measures procedure. If there is a significant difference among your groups, perform post hoc comparisons. Print the output.

3. Write a one- or two-sentence conclusion detailing the results and the meaning of your hypothesis test. Was there a significant difference among your groups? If so, which groups contributed to that difference?

ASSIGNMENT 8

Measuring the Simple Relationship Between Two Variables

OBJECTIVES

1. To formulate a research question focusing on the covariation between two variables

2. To produce a graph describing the relationship between the two variables

3. To provide an interpretation of the Pearson correlation

Correlation is a statistical technique that researchers use to explore the relationship between two variables. These variables are usually referred to as variable X and variable Y. The variables may exist naturally in the environment and are not necessarily manipulated by the researcher.

For example, suppose you are a sociologist interested in the relationship between education and income in the banking industry. The implied research question is, "What is the relationship between educational attainment and income in the banking industry?" Using data collected on a sample of individuals who work in the banking sector, you would use SPSS to calculate a Pearson correlation (r) between the two variables. By calculating the correlation between the two variables, you would learn about the strength of the relationship between the variables and about the direction of that relationship (i.e., positive or negative). As such, the correlation is sometimes referred to as a "measure of association." Values for correlations range from $r = -1.00$ to $r = +1.00$, indicating perfect negative and positive correlations, respectively. A correlation of $r = 0.00$ indicates absolutely no association between the variables. The absolute value of the range from 0 to 1 indicates the strength of the relationship between the two variables you have chosen.

CHOOSING THE Correlate PROCEDURE

After you have loaded your bank employee data (BANK.SAV in this example), you can proceed with the selection of a statistical procedure. If you click on the

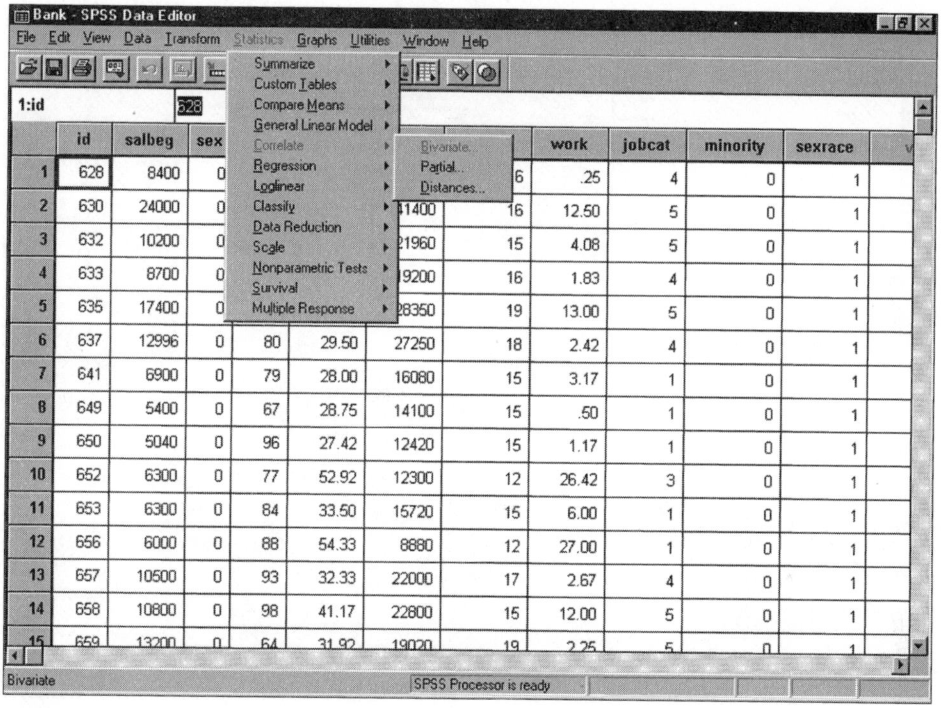

FIGURE 8.1 Accessing the Bivariate Correlation Procedure

Statistics pull-down menu, you will see a menu option labeled Correlate, as shown in Figure 8.1. Highlight the Correlate procedure and a sub-menu with another set of choices will pop up. Then click on the Bivariate option. (Note that SPSS will also calculate other forms of correlation such as partial correlations. Refer to your text for more information on these other types of correlational analysis.)

CHOOSING YOUR VARIABLES

In this procedure, you can assess the covariation between any two variables. The Correlate procedure will produce a correlation matrix showing the correlation between all possible pairings of the variables you choose. For example, if you choose two variables, SPSS will produce a 2 × 2 correlation matrix. The size of the matrix is directly related to the number of variables you choose.

Although you will need to choose only two variables for this assignment, you can choose more than the two required here. Remember to choose variables that are appropriate for the calculation of a Pearson correlation. For instance, the example used here assesses the relationship between educational attainment

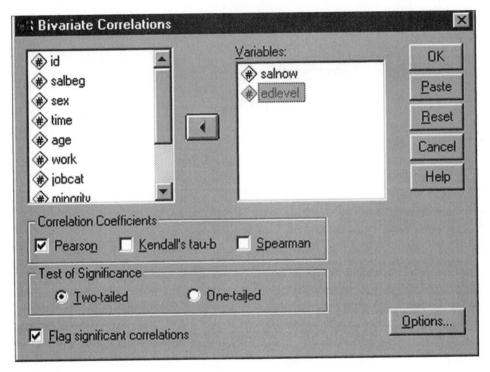

FIGURE 8.2   Selecting Variables for the Bivariate Correlation Procedure

(edlevel) and income (salnow). Both of these variables are measured on ratio scales. Variables measured on either interval or ratio scales of measure are appropriate variables to use in the calculation of a Pearson correlation.

After you select the Bivariate option, SPSS will produce the Bivariate Correlations window, as shown in Figure 8.2. This window is very similar to variable selection windows used in previous assignments. The left-hand box in this window contains all the variables in the datafile. You will need to choose two variables to complete the assignment. Note that the window does not discriminate between independent and dependent variables.

Figure 8.2 displays your choice of two variables from a file containing data about bank employees. You have chosen two variables, education (edlevel) and current salary (salnow), in order to investigate the relationship between educational attainment and income in the banking industry. The Bivariate Correlation procedure will produce a correlation matrix showing the correlation between these variables. Once you have chosen your variables and the type of correlation you wish to compute, click on the OK button. SPSS will process the requested statistics.

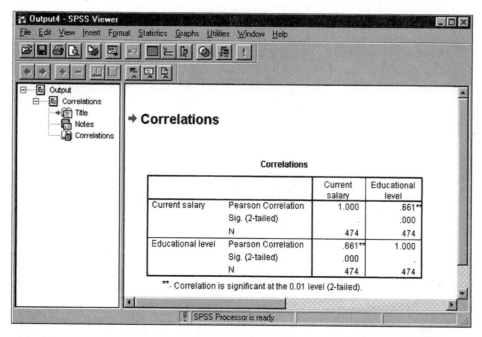

FIGURE 8.3   Output for the Pearson Correlation

Note two items in Figure 8.2. SPSS will calculate three different types of correlation for different types of data. The Spearman and Kendall correlation coefficients are used with data measured on nominal or ordinal scales. You will complete the assignment using the Pearson correlation coefficient.

SPSS also calculates both two-tailed and one-tailed tests of significance. Depending on how you have stated your hypothesis, you will choose either the one- or two-tailed test. When you click on the Flag significant correlations box, SPSS will calculate p values for each Pearson correlation and mark the significant correlations with asterisks (*). As in previous assignments, the p value is the actual probability of making a Type I error after rejecting the null hypothesis. You will reject or fail to reject your null hypothesis based on the criterion level you have stated for testing your hypothesis (usually $p = .05$ or $p = .01$).

Figure 8.3 shows the results of the test for this example. SPSS has calculated a correlation of $r = .661$ between educational attainment and income among bank employees. The positive correlation indicates a positive relationship between education and income. In other words, individuals with higher levels of education earn higher wages in the banking industry. Note the level of significance indicated on the correlation matrix (p value). Based on a conservative criterion of $p = .01$, the results indicate a significant positive correlation between education and income.

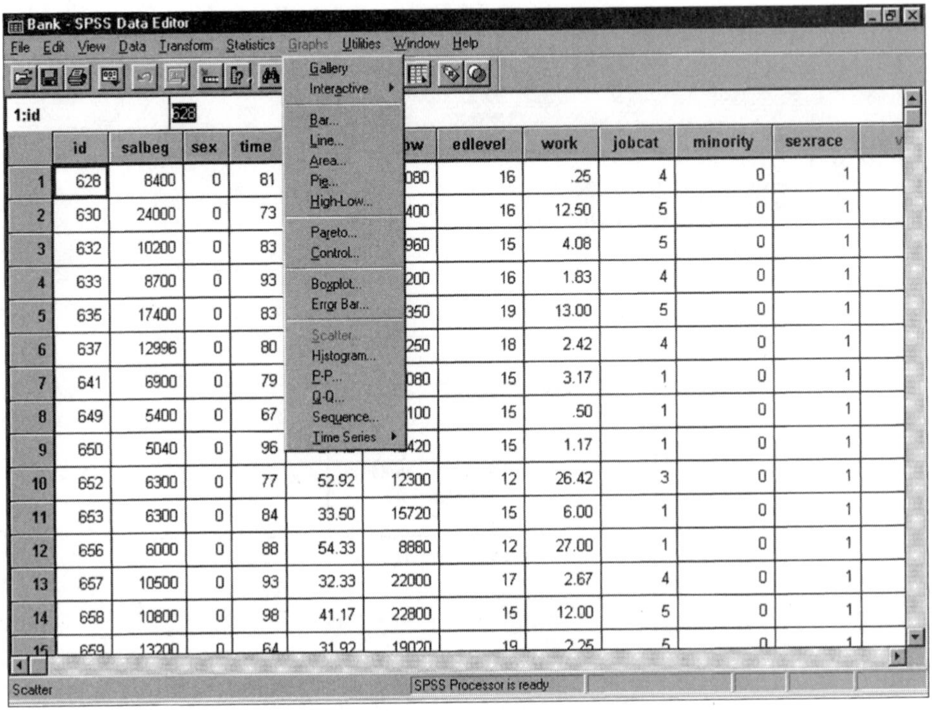

FIGURE 8.4   Choosing the Scatterplot Option

PLOTTING THE DATA

To graphically represent the association between two interval or ratio scale variables, researchers will plot the data using a scatterplot. The scatterplot will assist
you in a number of ways. First, the graphical representation will allow you to
acquire a better feeling for how the values of variable *X* covary with values of variable *Y*.

You will also be able to detect anomalies that reside in the data. For example,
you will detect what are called "outliers" in the data, or cases that, when plotted on
the scatterplot, appear distant from the clustering of most other cases. These types
of cases may have a profound impact on the correlation you are measuring.
Consequently, you will want to identify these cases as special cases upon which to
focus specific attention and perhaps eventually eliminate them from your analysis.

After you calculate the Pearson correlation in this assignment, you will produce a graph of the relationship between educational attainment and wages. Use
the Graphs pull-down menu from either the SPSS Viewer or the Data Editor and
select the Scatter option, as shown in Figure 8.4.

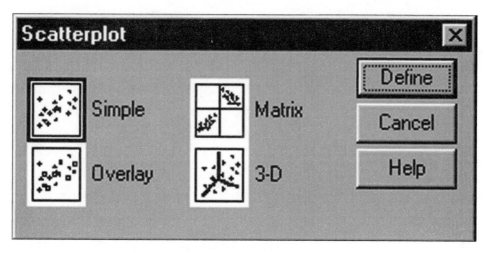

FIGURE 8.5   Choosing the Type of Scatterplot

The Scatter option is used to represent the relationship between your two variables in the form of a scatterplot. Measures from the two variables are plotted along both the X and Y axes as they occur together in the data. After you choose the Scatter option, SPSS will produce the Scatterplot window, as shown in Figure 8.5. Because you are plotting data along both the X and Y axes, you will click on the Simple option. Then click on the Define button to further define your request.

SPSS allows you to produce different types of scatterplots. You should experiment with the different types of plots to become familiar with the various methods of presenting correlative relationships between your variables. Choose the method of presentation that best describes the attributes of your data. Generally, scatterplots are very effective tools for the presentation of data related to the covariation between two variables measured on either interval or ratio scales of measure. Using a scatterplot to present data measured on either nominal or ordinal scales of measure will result in inaccurate presentations of the data.

Next, SPSS will produce the Simple Scatterplot window, as shown in Figure 8.6. Among other things, this window allows you to choose the variables you wish to plot. In this example, choose the same variables used in the calculation of the Pearson correlation. Click on the OK button, and SPSS will produce the scatterplot in the right-hand pane of your SPSS Viewer window, as shown in Figure 8.7.

If the scatterplot is satisfactory, you can print it using the Print function listed in the File pull-down menu in the SPSS Viewer. The processing of the chart for printing takes significant computer resources, so for slower computers, it may take several minutes to print the graphic. Note the Titles and Options buttons shown in

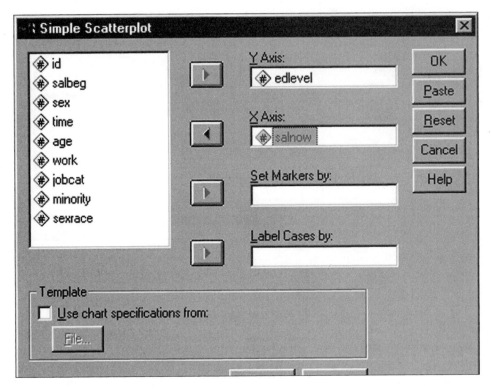

FIGURE 8.6   Choosing Variables for the Scatterplot

Figure 8.6. You can use these functions to embellish your scatterplot for purposes of presentation. SPSS will also export graphics to a number of commonly used file formats for storing graphical information.

ON YOUR OWN

You are now ready to explore the relationship between two variables on your own. To complete this task, do the following:

1. State your research questions and related hypotheses.

2. Test your hypotheses using the Correlate procedure.

3. Produce a scatterplot describing the covariation between the two variables you have chosen.

4. Summarize your findings in a brief descriptive paragraph.

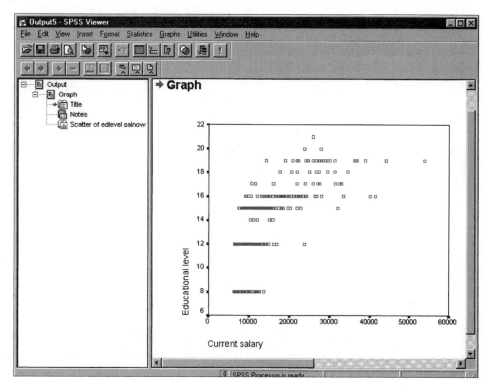

FIGURE 8.7 Output Showing the Scatterplot of Education Level and Current Salary

ASSIGNMENT 9

Describing the Linear Relationship Between Two Variables

OBJECTIVES

1. To understand the relationship between correlation and regression

2. To formulate a research question predicting the impact of one or more independent variables on the dependent variable

3. To use SPSS to compute the regression coefficient(s)

4. To summarize the results of the Regression procedure

In Assignment 8, you learned about measuring the relationship between two variables using the Pearson correlation. You also produced a scatterplot of the X and Y coordinates that described the covariation between the two variables.

In this assignment, you will focus on the description of the relationship between X and Y variables using regression procedures. Regression statistical techniques attempt to find the best way of describing the relationship between the dependent variable and one or more independent variables using a regression line. The regression line represents the "best-fitting" straight line projected through a set of X-Y coordinates like those you produced in the scatterplot in Assignment 8.

Researchers refer to the dependent variable as Y and to the independent variable as X. As in a correlation analysis, each case in a regression study has a value for both Y and X. When describing the relationship between X and Y, researchers often speak of X as predicting Y. The general mathematical expression for this relationship is as follows:

$$\hat{Y} = a + bX$$

where

$\hat{Y}$ = the predicted value for the dependent variable Y

X = the value for the independent variable X

b = the regression coefficient (i.e., the slope of the regression line)

a = the value of the Y intercept (i.e., the point on the Y axis through which the regression line traverses)

64

In this assignment, you will be introduced to how SPSS produces output for two forms of regression analysis: bivariate regression and multiple regression. Bivariate regression analysis involves describing the relationship between the dependent variable Y and one independent variable X. Multiple regression involves describing the relationship between the dependent variable Y and more than one independent variable $(X_1, X_2, X_3,$ etc.$)$. In the multiple regression analysis, you can employ multiple independent variables to simultaneously predict the dependent variable. The advantage of multiple regression techniques is that they allow you to predict the dependent variable in a more comprehensive manner using information from many variables at the same time.

The resulting mathematical expression for the multiple regression technique with two independent variables is as follows:

$$\hat{Y} = a + b_1 X_1 + b_2 X_2$$

where

$\hat{Y}$ = the predicted value for the dependent variable Y

X_1 = the value for the first independent variable X_1

X_2 = the value for the second independent variable X_2

b_1 = the regression coefficient for the first independent variable X_1

b_2 = the regression coefficient for the second independent variable X_2

a = the value of the Y intercept (i.e., the point on the Y axis through which the regression line traverses)

THE RESEARCH QUESTION

Research questions posed in the context of regression techniques are very similar to those posed in the context of the Pearson correlation. In Assignment 8, the research question was, "What is the relationship between educational attainment and income in the banking industry?" SPSS output suggested a strong positive correlation ($r = .661$) between the two variables. Given this strong correlation, you might ask, "How does educational attainment predict salary in the banking industry?" Implicit in the question is the notion that educational attainment will predict employee salaries. Regression analysis is an appropriate statistical technique to use in answering such a question. Furthermore, regression analysis allows you to assess the impact of multiple factors as implied by the question, "How does educational attainment predict salary in the banking industry apart from the age of the employee?" This question queries the impact of education upon salary, simultaneously recognizing that the age of employees may also have an impact. And to answer the question, you must use multiple regression techniques. In both scenarios, the dependent measure is the salary of the employees. Independent variables are the educational attainment and the age of employees.

In the Pearson correlation, the strength and direction of the relationship between X and Y were based on the size and sign of the correlation (r). In regression analysis, the impact of the independent variable(s) on the dependent variable is assessed in a similar manner using the coefficient of each variable. The larger the coefficient, the larger the effect on the dependent variable Y in either a positive or negative direction. Independent variables with coefficients with values near zero have little effect on Y. It is helpful to think of the coefficient as having a multiplier effect on Y. In other words, for every one unit change in X, there is an X times b unit change in Y. Given a value for X, the size of the coefficient b allows you to predict the resulting change in Y.

The goal of multiple regression techniques is to use the multiple independent variables to explain as much of the variation in the dependent variable as possible. Ideally, adding more independent variables to the equation will increase the amount of variation in Y "predicted" by the independent variables. The amount of variation explained by the independent variables is known as the coefficient of determination, or r^2. Here, r^2 measures the percentage of variation explained by the independent variables.

Although you can think of independent variables within the regression equation as "predicting" the dependent variable, you must be careful not to assume that a causal linkage occurs between the independent and dependent variables. In many analytic scenarios, regression analysis represents a more complex form of correlation analysis. Consequently, the presence of a relationship between an independent variable and a dependent variable merely denotes association, and not necessarily causality.

CHOOSING THE Regression PROCEDURE

You will continue using the bank employee example for this assignment. After you have loaded your bank employee data (BANK.SAV in this example), select the Regression procedure. Once you click on the Statistics pull-down menu, you will see an option on the menu labeled Regression, as shown in Figure 9.1. After highlighting Regression, a sub-menu will appear. Note that you are given several options on this menu. While some installations may allow users to access advanced regression techniques (e.g., logistic regression), all users should have access to both the Linear and Curve Estimation options.

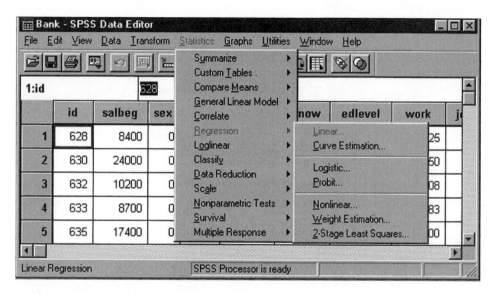

FIGURE 9.1   Choosing the Linear Regression Procedure

CHOOSING YOUR VARIABLES

To choose your variables, you will need to access the Linear Regression window. After you click on Linear, SPSS will produce the Linear Regression window, as shown in Figure 9.2. This window allows you to choose both your dependent and independent variables. As in previous assignments, click on your chosen variables and then click on the appropriate arrow button to place the variable in either the dependent or independent variable boxes. Note that the dependent variable box allows you to insert only one variable while the independent variable box allows you to insert more than one variable. You will insert one independent variable for bivariate regression and more than one independent variable for multiple regression,

The Linear Regression window allows you to do several tasks related to both basic and advanced regression analysis. For this assignment, you will perform only the most basic tasks related to regression analysis. This involves having SPSS produce some descriptive statistics about the variables you are choosing. First, click on the Statistics button in the Linear Regression window. SPSS will produce the Linear Regression: Statistics window, as shown in Figure 9.3. You will choose the Estimates, Descriptives, and Model fit statistics from this menu by clicking on each of the choices.

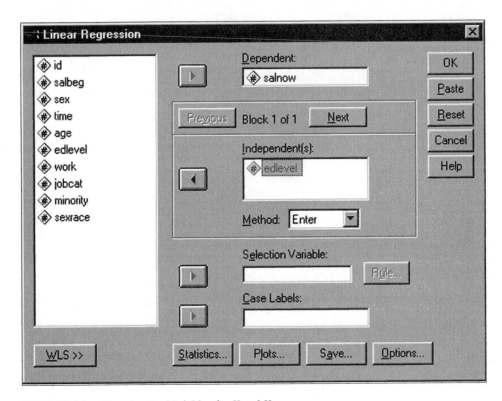

FIGURE 9.2   Choosing the Variables for *X* and *Y*

After you choose the statistics, click on the Continue button, and the Linear Regression window will reappear. Click on the OK button, and SPSS will calculate the regression output for this analysis.

INTERPRETING THE OUTPUT

In this assignment, two regression analyses are requested. The first analysis is a bivariate regression analysis using salnow (salary) as the dependent variable and edlevel (educational attainment) as the independent variable. This type of model represents regression analysis in its simplest form. The second analysis is a multiple regression analysis and involves more than one independent variable.

In the first analysis, you use salary as the dependent variable. Salary is being predicted by the independent variable educational attainment. Since the correlation between these two variables was found to be positive in Assignment 8, you should expect to find a positive regression coefficient for educational attainment.

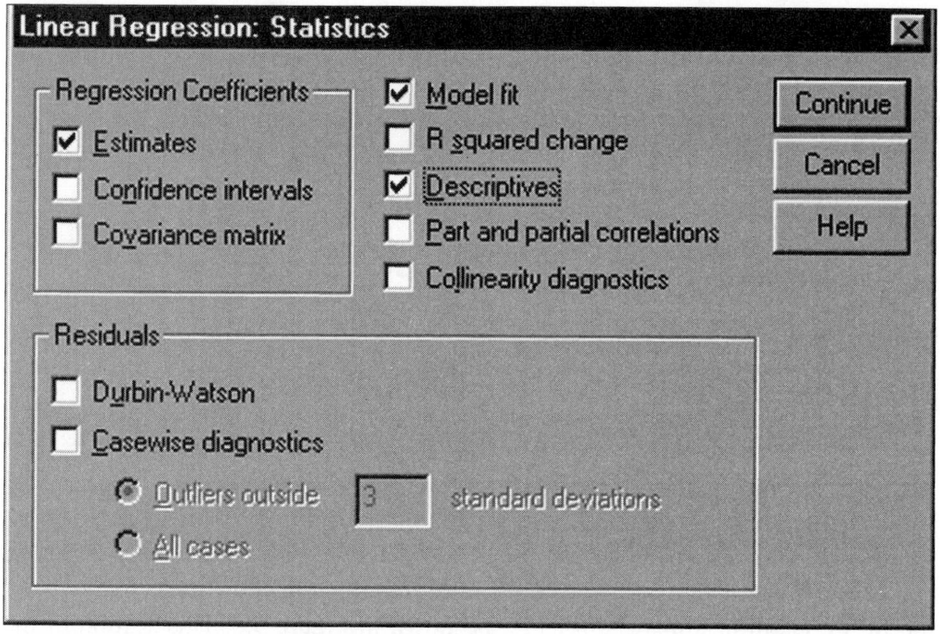

FIGURE 9.3 Choosing Statistics for the Regression Procedure

In the second analysis, you are also interested in the effect that age may have on salary. It is reasonable to assume that older bank employees have higher salaries because they have worked longer and probably have achieved promotions throughout their careers. To assess the simultaneous impact of educational attainment and age on salary for bank employees, add the age variable to the second analysis. SPSS produces output for both of the analyses.

Bivariate Regression

For this assignment, you need to focus on three types of information produced by SPSS and shown by the SPSS Viewer. The first item to note is the coefficient of determination, designated as R Square (r^2) as shown in Figure 9.4. In this example, the r^2 value is .436. This indicates that approximately 44 percent of the variation in salaries is explained by educational attainment.

You also need to note the F statistic, shown as $F = 365.381$ in Figure 9.5. F is the value calculated for the F statistic by SPSS (or the F ratio for the regression equation). The significance value (Sig.) is the computed likelihood of committing a Type I error after rejecting the null hypothesis. In this case, Sig. = .000 ($p < .001$), which is less than $p < .05$ (the criterion alpha level). Therefore, you can conclude that the regression equation as computed is statistically significant.

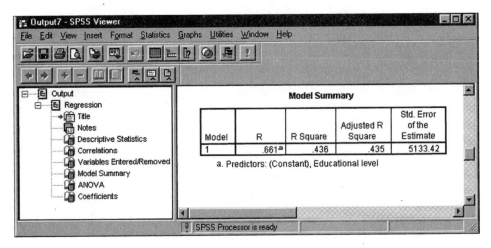

FIGURE 9.4   Bivariate Regression Output Showing the Coefficient of Determination

In regression analysis, however, the most important information is found under the SPSS output heading Coefficients, as shown in Figure 9.6. This section of the output shows you which of the variables were statistically significant predictors of the dependent variable. There are three critical components in this section:

B   the unstandardized regression coefficient

Beta   the standardized coefficient (Beta in this example is .661 and is equal to the Pearson correlation computed in Assignment 8.)

Sig.   the computed probability for making a Type I error for the independent variable edlevel

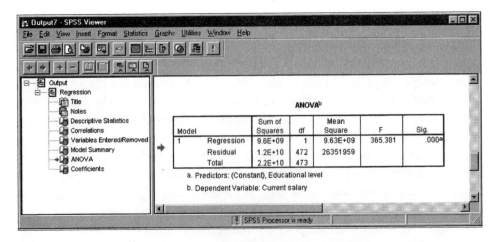

FIGURE 9.5   Bivariate Regression Output Showing the ANOVA for the Regression

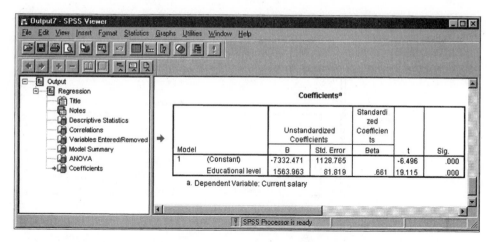

FIGURE 9.6   Significance of Predictor Variables in the Bivariate Regression Analysis

In this case, Sig. = .000 ($p < .001$), which is less than $p < .05$ (the criterion alpha level). You can conclude, then, that educational attainment is a significant predictor of salary for banking employees because Sig. is less than the alpha level designated for the analysis.

Multiple Regression

In the multiple regression output, note that the age variable is included in the Coefficients section of the output shown in Figure 9.7. When you examine the output, you will find that age is not a significant predictor of salary because Sig. is greater than the criterion alpha level of .05 (i.e., .233 > .05). This is a case in which a nonsignificant result is still useful, because it eliminates a potential explanation for the variation found in the salaries of bank employees. By using multiple regression, you have taken into account more than one explanation for that variation. (In an analysis of this type, you may want to consider including (as independent variables) all the variables you think might have an effect on your dependent variable.) *Do this.*

ON YOUR OWN

You are now ready to use the Regression procedure to further assess patterns of covariation in your data. To complete this task, do the following:

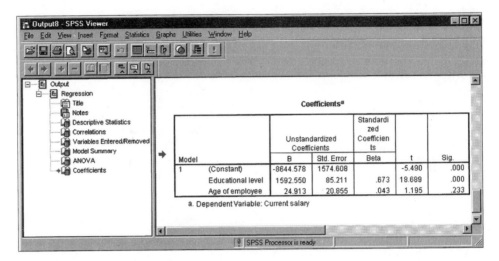

FIGURE 9.7 Significance of Predictor Variables in the Multiple Regression Analysis

1. Formulate a research question appropriate for use with regression analysis.

2. Use SPSS to perform both a bivariate and a multivariate regression analysis using at least two independent variables.

3. Describe the results of your regression analysis in the form of a brief analysis of each of your independent variables.

ASSIGNMENT 10

Assessing the Association Between Two Categorical Variables

OBJECTIVES

1. To formulate a research question focusing on the association between two variables

2. To use the SPSS Crosstabs procedure to produce contingency tables

3. To use SPSS to compute the chi-square statistic

4. To describe the results of the chi-square statistic

Researchers often face situations in which their data are not measured using interval or ratio scales of measure. They also face situations in which their data are not normally distributed. In such situations, researchers must utilize a family of statistics referred to as "nonparametric" statistics. Nonparametric statistics differ from parametric statistics such as independent-samples *t* tests in that nonparametric tests do not require the researcher to make assumptions about the normal distribution of the data and homogeneity of variance. Researchers use these tests in situations in which the data do not meet the assumptions of normality and homogeneity of variance. Given the characteristics of the nonparametric tests, this family of statistics is well suited for use with data measured on nominal or ordinal scales.

In this assignment, you will begin to use the chi-square statistic (χ^2), a nonparametric statistic. When using parametric statistics, you are comparing population parameters such as the mean or standard deviation. When using the chi-square statistic, you are interested in learning about differences in proportion or frequency as they occur between two populations. A research question suggesting such a comparison might be, "How does the number of male and female pilots in the airline industry compare relative to the number of males and females in the general population?" In this situation, you would use the chi-square statistic to assess the differences in the proportion of men and women as they occur in the population of airline pilots relative to the general population. Sometimes this type of test is referred to as the chi-square test for goodness-of-fit.

In other situations, you might use a statistical test to ascertain whether a relationship exists between two variables measured using a nominal or ordinal scale of measure. In this analytic scenario, you would use the chi-square test for independence. A research question dictating this type of a test might be, "Does the proportion of male and female pilots vary between airline companies?" This question would require you to examine the proportion of male and female pilots across the major airlines to ascertain whether differences exist in the proportions of male and female pilots, company by company. If you used the chi-square statistic to evaluate this question, finding different proportions between the airline companies would mean that a relationship does exist between the variables of sex and airline company. In other words, the proportion of male and female pilots depends on the airline company. Conversely, finding the same proportions across the airline companies would indicate that no relationship exists between the variables.

In this assignment, you will learn how to use the SPSS Crosstabs procedure to calculate the chi-square test for independence. SPSS will construct crosstabulations (i.e., contingency or cross-classification tables) between the classifications (categories) of two variables. The crosstabulation takes the form of a frequency distribution arranged as a matrix in which rows correspond to the categories of one variable and columns correspond to the categories of the second variable. From the intersection of rows and columns emerge cells that represent both.

To calculate the chi-square statistic, SPSS must calculate both expected and observed frequencies as they occur in each cell. Observed frequencies are the actual frequencies that emerge as the result of your cross-classification of the two variables. Expected frequencies are those the researcher would expect if there were no relationship between the two variables.

To calculate the chi-square statistic, SPSS examines the cumulative magnitude of difference between the expected and observed frequencies in each cell. (Refer to your text for the formula for the chi-square statistic.) As the cumulative magnitude of difference between observed and expected cells increases across the cells, the value of the chi-square statistic becomes larger. As the chi-square statistic increases, the likelihood increases that a relationship exists between the two variables.

Prior to performing the Crosstabs procedure, you must specify a research question and state a set of hypotheses to be tested using the chi-square statistic. In the example used here, suppose you are using General Social Survey data from 1991 to examine the relationship between sex and view of life. The implicit research question is, "Is there a relationship between sex and an individual's overall view of life?" To properly evaluate the query posed by the research question, you must state the question in the form of hypotheses. (Refer to your textbook for more about hypothesis testing.) After stating the hypotheses, you will be ready to actually test them using the chi-square test for independence.

PERFORMING THE Crosstabs PROCEDURE

After loading your data, use the Statistics pull-down menu to access the Crosstabs procedure. This procedure is accessed by clicking on Summarize and then highlighting the Crosstabs option from the Statistics pull-down window (i.e., Statistics>Summarize>Crosstabs), as shown in Figure 10.1. (Note that the sub-menu listing Crosstabs appears to the right of the main Statistics pull-down menu. This occurs as a function of the Statistics menu position relative to the size of the SPSS Data Editor window open as shown.)

After you access the Crosstabs procedure, SPSS will produce the Crosstabs window. The Crosstabs window lists all variables in the left-hand pane, as shown in Figure 10.2. You will need to choose one variable to appear as a row in the Crosstabs table and another variable to appear as a column. In the present example, you are interested in examining the relationship between the variables of sex and view of life. You have placed the sex variable in the row box and the life view variable in the column box. Note that the Crosstabs table will allow you to insert a third variable into the Layer 1 of 1 box. Insertion of a variable here instructs SPSS to produce a three-way contingency table comparing three different categories of variables.

After choosing your variables, you must indicate that the chi-square statistic will be calculated by the Crosstabs procedure. Choose the chi-square statistic by clicking on the Statistics button appearing in the Crosstabs window to produce the window shown in Figure 10.3. Although the Crosstabs: Statistics window provides a number of statistical options, you will select only the chi-square statistic for this exercise. After selecting Chi-square, click on the Continue button, and the Crosstabs window will reappear.

To complete the analysis, you also need to click on the Cells button in the main Crosstabs window. SPSS will produce the Crosstabs: Cell Display window with a number of options. To understand the crosstabulation of the two variables, you should select those options shown in Figure 10.4. These are the Observed and Expected Counts and the Row and Column Percentages. These options will provide the detail needed to understand the chi-square statistic. Once you have chosen your cell attributes, click on the Continue button. The Crosstabs window will reappear. After you click on the OK button in the Crosstabs window, SPSS will produce the contingency table and calculate the chi-square statistic.

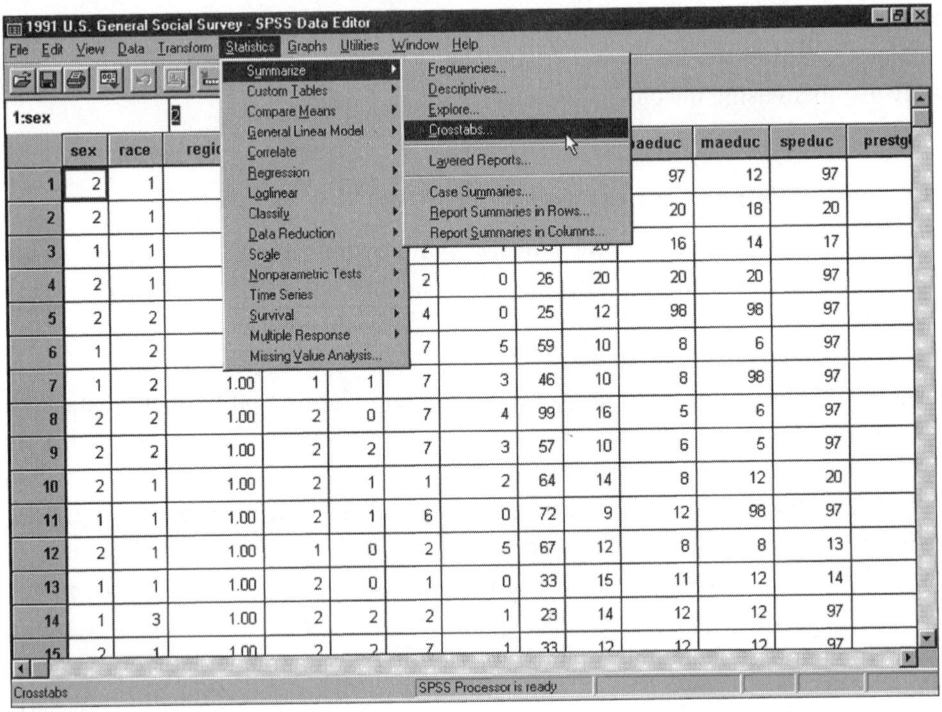

FIGURE 10.1   Accessing the Crosstabs Procedure

INTERPRETING THE Chi-Square AND Crosstabs OUTPUT

As stated previously, the Crosstabs procedure produces a contingency table of two cross-classified variables. To understand the chi-square statistic, you may find it helpful to focus on the observed values and expected values in the cells of the contingency table. You may also want to focus on the "proportionality" between cells in the table. It is the difference between the values in each cell that determines the size of the calculated chi-square statistic. Large differences will produce large values of chi-square, and vice versa. Independence between the two variables is assumed as a function of the size of the chi-square statistic. Statistically significant values of chi-square denote association between the two variables, whereas nonsignificant values of chi-square denote independence between the two variables.

You should be cautious in making evaluations about the chi-square statistic in situations in which cells have fewer than five observations. In such cases, SPSS will produce a warning about small cell sizes. The calculation of the chi-square statistic is affected by very small observed frequencies in cells and may provide misleading information about the relationship between the two variables.

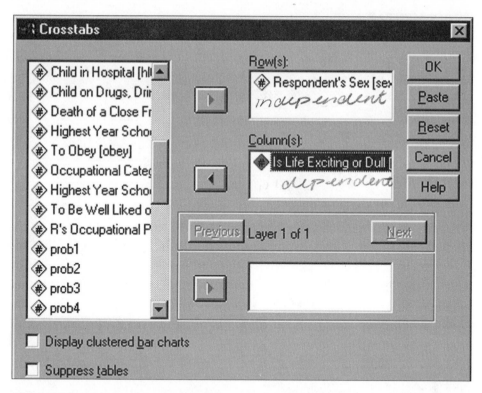

FIGURE 10.2 Choosing the Variables for the Crosstabs Procedure

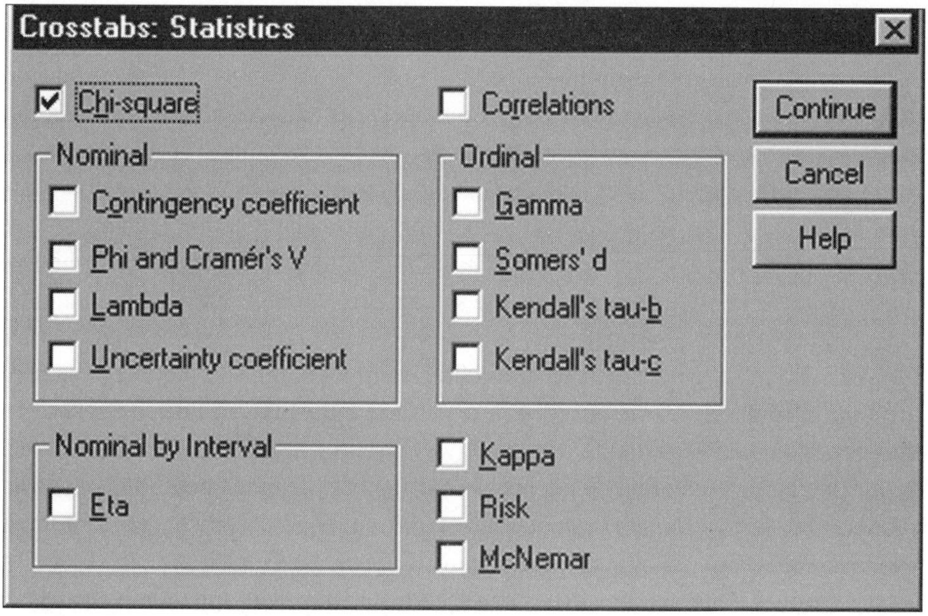

FIGURE 10.3 Choosing the Chi-Square Statistic

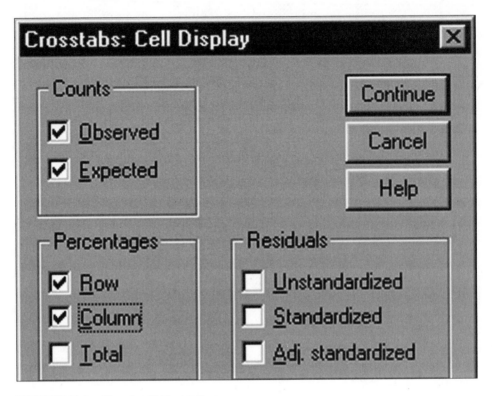

FIGURE 10.4   Choosing Table Attributes

Figure 10.5 shows the output appearing in the SPSS Viewer window produced by the Crosstabs procedure. The output includes a contingency table showing the various possible categories of response across the two variables. The categories of response for the life variable include Dull, Routine, and Exciting. The row percentages are indicated as the % within Respondents's Sex. The column percentages are indicated as % within Is Life Exciting or Dull. To gain a more comprehensive understanding of the relationship between the sex and life variables, however, you must examine the degree to which the counts (observed) and expected counts within each cell differ. Large differences are indicative of a relationship between the way men and women view life. Small differences are indicative of little difference in their sentiments toward life.

Although you may find differences occurring between the counts and expected counts, you must obtain a calculation of the chi-square statistic to determine whether an overall statistically significant difference exists. Figure 10.6 shows results from the calculation of the chi-square statistic as it appears in the SPSS Viewer window. The calculated p value for the chi-square statistic is shown as the

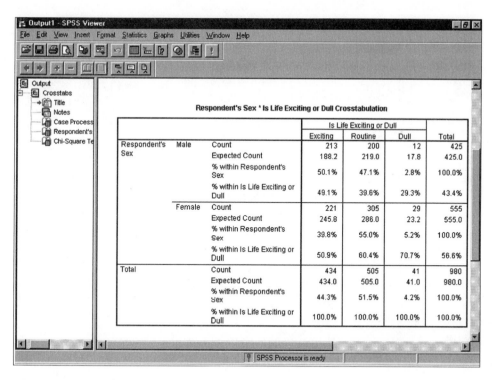

FIGURE 10.5   SPSS Output of the Crosstabs Procedure

Asymp. Sig. (2-sided) calculation. As in previous assignments, you reject or fail to reject your null hypothesis based on the alpha level you have chosen (usually $p = .05$ or $p = .01$). In other words, Asymp. Sig. (2-sided) refers to the likelihood of making a Type I error if you choose to reject the null hypothesis. In this example, the Asymp. Sig. (2-sided) value is less than $p = .05$, indicating that men and women have different views on life.

Note that you are using the Pearson chi-square as shown in Figure 10.6. This refers not to the Pearson correlation, but rather to a method of calculating the chi-square statistic. The Value column as shown in the output is the chi-square value as calculated by SPSS. Similarly, df refers to the degrees of freedom.

ON YOUR OWN

You are now ready to use SPSS to construct contingency tables and to calculate the chi-square statistic to assess the association between two categorical variables. To complete this task, do the following:

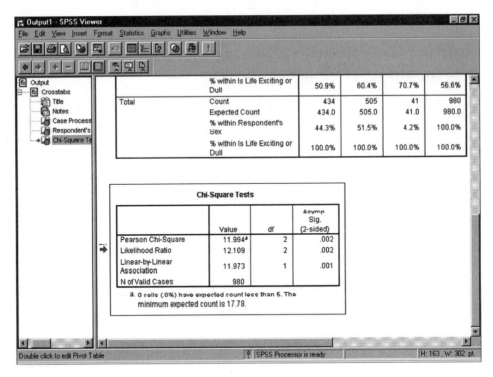

FIGURE 10.6　SPSS Output of the Chi-Square Statistic

1. State your research question based on two variables in your datafile.

2. Test your hypotheses using the chi-square statistic.

3. Summarize your findings in a descriptive paragraph about your analysis.

APPENDIX

Entering Data Using Programs Other Than SPSS

USING A TEXT EDITOR TO ENTER DATA

You can use any text editor or word processor to enter data. Data may have to adhere exactly to a specific format and must be saved in ASCII (text) form. The following data formats can be used when entering data with a text editor:

Fixed

Freefield

Tab delimited

The fixed and freefield formats are remnants of the era of punchcard and paper tape data entry, but they form the basis of today's more sophisticated data entry procedures.

FIXED FORMAT

In fixed format, the data for each participant (case) is entered on a line (record). If there is too much data to enter on a single line, more records may be allotted to each case. There will always be the same number of records in each case even if they are not needed for some cases.

Each numeric digit, alphabetic character, or symbol that constitutes your variable will occupy a specific column in a particular record. For example, if you start at the left margin of the page, and the subject ID number "8953" is the first variable you enter, it will occupy columns 1, 2, 3, and 4 in record 1 of each case.

Numeric variables can be 40 columns wide, and string variables (text) can be up to 255 columns wide. A record can contain up to 1024 columns. Because the specific columns containing data are defined the same way for each case, you can choose not to leave spaces between the variables. This saves space on the record but sacrifices readability.

You can use any simple text editor (such as the Windows Notepad) or a sophisticated word processor (such as Microsoft Word or WordPerfect) to generate the fixed-format datafile. Make sure that column numbering starts from the left margin and that there are no blank lines at the beginning or end of the file. You must save the output from the text editor or word processor in ASCII (text) form. If you save the file with the extension .dat, SPSS will automatically recognize it as a datafile.

Two samples of data entered in fixed format follow.

Sample A

The variables ID, age, gender, and score are entered in fixed format with a space between each variable. There are four cases with one record each.

```
_____    <—Top of page
8953  22  F    95
8954      M  90
8955  20  F    91
8960  24  M  97  <—Last line
```

The variables are found in the following columns: ID = 1–4, age = 6–7, gender = 9, score = 11–12. Note that gender is a string variable and that age is missing for the second case.

Sample B

The same data are entered without spaces.

```
_____    <—Top of page
895322F95
8954  M90
895520F91
896024M97  <—Last line
```

In Sample B, the variables are in the following columns: ID = 1–4, age = 5–6, gender = 7, score = 8–9.

In fixed format, variable names and decimal points are not contained in the datafile, but instead are specified in the process of loading the datafile into SPSS. If a case has missing values, simply leave the space allotted to that variable blank.

Loading a Fixed-Format File into SPSS

From the menu bar, choose File>Read ASCII Data>Fixed Columns. You will be asked to provide the filename, variable names, and variable type, and the column assignments for each variable. It is generally helpful if you have written this information down when you set up your data entry format. If you have any problems, consult the Help menu.

FREEFIELD FORMAT

In freefield format, there must be at least one space between the data points for each variable. You can insert more than one space between variables, but there must not be spaces within a variable. String variables are the exception and may contain spaces if the entire string is enclosed in single quotes.

When loading freefield data, you first tell SPSS the names of the variables in the order that they are entered. You must also provide the maximum length of each string variable. When SPSS reads your freefield datafile, it reads each number or string entered and assigns them serially to the variables for the first case. When the value corresponding to the last variable for the first case is reached, SPSS reads the next value and assigns it to the first variable of the second case, and so on. This means that when you enter the data for each case, you must enter a value for each variable. If data is missing for a case, you can use a period to represent the missing data. You can also choose a special value for missing data. Make sure that the value you choose is not one that is representative of real data. You will define that special value to mean missing data after the file has been loaded by SPSS. SPSS will set that value to the system-missing value. Note that you will receive warning messages when that happens.

Two samples of data entered in freefield format follow.

Sample A

The variables ID, age, gender, and score are entered in freefield format with a space between each variable. There are four cases with one record each.

```
———————————————————    <—Top of page
8953 22 F 95
8954 . M 90
8955 20 F 91
8960 24 M 97   <—Last line
```

Note that this arrangement is exactly the same as the first fixed-format sample except for the treatment of missing values.

Sample B

The same data are all entered on the same line.

```
_____   <—Top of page
8953 22 F 95 8954 . M 90 8955 20 F 91 8960 24 M 97 <—Last line
```

SPSS will read Sample B in the same way as Sample A. However, it may be harder for you to read and interpret a printout of the raw datafile when it is structured as in Sample B.

Loading a Freefield Format File into SPSS

From the menu bar, choose File>Read ASCII Data>Freefield. You will be asked to provide the filename, variable names, and variable type, and the maximum length of string variables. You will receive noncritical (ignorable) warnings about any missing values you have entered. If you have any problems, consult the Help menu.

TAB-DELIMITED FORMAT

In the tab-delimited format, variable names are entered on the first line of the datafile and are read directly by SPSS. The variable names and the data themselves are separated into columns using the Tab key. Missing data are defined in the same way as for freefield format.

Here is a sample of data entered in tab-delimited format:

```
_____   <—Top of page

ID     AGE   GENDER  SCORE
8953   22    F       95
8954   .     M       90
8955   20    F       91
8960   24    M       97          <—Last line
```

Loading a Tab-Delimited Format File into SPSS

To load a tab-delimited format file into SPSS, do the following:

1. From the menu bar, choose File>Open.

2. Enter the filename.

3. Choose Tab-delimited (*.dat) under the Files of type: drop list.

4. Click on the Open button.

5. Click on the Read variable names check-box.

6. Click on the OK button.

You will receive noncritical warnings about any missing values you have entered. If you have any problems, consult the Help menu.

USING A SPREADSHEET TO ENTER DATA

SPSS will read data directly from Microsoft Excel and Lotus 123 files. Spreadsheet data entry is similar to that in the tab-delimited format. Variables are arranged in columns, and cases are represented by rows. Variable names can be entered in the first row of the data set. Here is a sample of data entered in spreadsheet format:

```
ID     AGE  GENDER  SCORE  <— First row of spreadsheet
8953   22   F       95
8954        M       90
8955   20   F       91
8960   24   M       97
```

In this sample, the ID variable for the first participant (case) occupies cell A1 in the spreadsheet, while the SCORE variable for the fourth participant (case) occupies cell D5. You can use these cell addresses to specify a range of data to load into SPSS. For example, if you wanted only the ID number and the age for each participant, you could load only the range of scores from A1 to B5. SPSS treats empty cells (as for AGE in cell B3) as missing data.

Loading Data from a Spreadsheet into SPSS

To load data from a spreadsheet into SPSS, do the following:

1. From the menu bar, choose: File>Open.

2. Enter the filename.

3. Choose Excel (*.xls) or Lotus (*.w*) under the Files of type: drop list.

4. Click on the Open button.

5. Click on the Read variable names check-box.

6. Enter a range of data to load if necessary.

7. Click on the OK button.

You will receive noncritical warnings about any missing values you have entered. If you have any problems, consult the Help menu.

USING A DATABASE TO ENTER DATA

SPSS will read data from any database program that produces dBASE (.DBF) files. Field names are read as variable names. If you are creating the database solely for the purpose of data entry, we recommend that you use variable names no longer than eight characters. If the field name is longer than eight characters, SPSS truncates it to eight. And if truncation produces duplicate variable names, duplicate variables are dropped!

Loading Data from a Database into SPSS

To load data from a database into SPSS, do the following:

1. From the menu bar, choose: File>Open.
2. Enter the filename.
3. Choose dBASE (.dbf) under the Files of type: drop list.
4. Click on the Open button.

If you have any problems, consult the Help menu.

USING DATABASE CAPTURE WIZARD

The Database Capture Wizard allows retrieval of data from programs that use the ODBC (Open DataBase Connectivity) protocol. ODBC compliant data sources include Microsoft Access and Excel.

The Database Capture Wizard can be accessed from the SPSS opening dialog box described in Assignment 1 (see Figure 1.4) by selecting the Create new query using Database Capture Wizard option. It can also be started from the SPSS File menu by choosing the Database Capture option. The Database Capture Wizard operates by using a simple question-answer format. The following example shows how to retrieve data from a Microsoft Access database file using the Database Capture Wizard.

Loading Data from an Access File into SPSS

To load data from an Access file into SPSS, do the following:

1. From the menu bar, choose File>Database Capture>New Query.
2. At the initial Database Capture Wizard screen, click on MS Access 7.0 Database and then click on the Next> button.

3. Select the directory that contains your Access file in the Directories box to the right, and then click on the appropriate filename in the Database Name box on the left. Click on the OK button.

4. To move all the fields in the database into SPSS, simply click and drag the entire table from the box on the left to the box on the right. To select a subset of fields from the data table, expand the table in the left box by clicking on the + to the left of the table name. Click and drag the desired fields from the left box to the right box. When all the fields have been selected, click on the Next> button. Note that from this point on, you have the option of clicking on the Finish button if you do not need to further process the data in the fields you have selected.

5. You can now limit or filter the values of each of the fields you selected in step 4. After this is completed, continue by clicking on Next>.

6. You can add or change the variable names in the fifth screen. Click on Next> to continue.

7. The last screen displays the data query in SPSS syntax. You must run this query to load your data. To load the selected data, click on Finish. You can also save the query in an SPSS *.spq file by typing a filename in the Save query to file box. Using a saved query speeds up the query process. The next time you want to load this same data, choose File>Database Capture>Run Query from the menu bar.